Mr. Leroy Neal
6217 Robin Hill Rd
Baltimore, MD 21207-6261

SURVIVING THE
SHAKING

Other books by Keavin Hayden:

Lifestyles of the Remnant
Saving Blood
The Shaking Among God's People
Truth That Matters

To order, call 1-800-765-6955.
Visit us at www.reviewandherald.com for information
on other Review and Herald® products.

SURVIVING THE
SHAKING

Keavin Hayden

REVIEW AND HERALD® PUBLISHING ASSOCIATION
HAGERSTOWN, MD 21740

The author assumes full responsibility for the accuracy of all facts and quotations as cited in this book.

This book was
Edited by Gerald Wheeler
Copyedited by Lori Halvorsen and James Cavil
Cover designed by Trent Truman
Electronic makeup by Shirley M. Bolivar
Type: 12/14 Bembo

PRINTED IN U.S.A.
06 05 04 03 02   5 4 3 2 1

R&H Cataloging Service

Hayden, Ronald Keavin, 1960-
    Another shaking among God's people.

    1. Seventh-day Adventists—Revival and Reformation.   2. Justification.
3. Seventh-day Adventists—Doctrines.   4. Perfection—Religious Aspects.
5. Sanctification.   I. Title.

286.732

ISBN 0-8280-1643-7

DEDICATION

To all the administrators, leaders, and teachers of this denomination, whose dedication and hard work advance the vision of Seventh-day Adventism around the world. May the Head of this church, our Lord and Savior Jesus Christ, continue to strengthen and bless each one of you in your ministry of lifting Him up to the world.

CONTENTS

INTRODUCTION

Shortly after joining the Seventh-day Adventist Church in 1984, I met a man who quickly became a major influence in my life. Not having had any historical background in Adventism, I naturally began to look at this new friend, whom we will call Jim, as a kind of mentor. But his influence soon led me down a path that would take years to backtrack.

To begin with, Jim was heavily involved in a works-oriented religion. Again and again he emphasized that only the obedient would be saved. He assured me that God required us to be radically different from everyone else, even among Adventists, and stated that it would be the peculiarity that would give my witness unusual power.

Having been raised a Baptist, such a perspective on obedience was new to me. I had been taught that all you had to do was "just believe" that Jesus loves you and died for your sins. But the fact that multitudes of mainstream denominations refused to comply with obedience to the Sabbath commandment caused me to regard my earlier training as being "cheap grace"-oriented. *Jim's right,* I thought to myself; *the whole of Christendom is going to hell in the devil's hand-basket, because they place too much emphasis on grace. Even the Adventists are falling short in adhering to all that God requires of them through the teachings of Ellen White.* Thus a more legalistic approach to salvation subtly crept into my reasoning.

This prepared the way for what Jim would next tell me. One day he choked up with tears and informed me that the Lord had laid a heavy burden upon his heart for Adventism, the denomination of his youth. "Our beloved church," he said, "is heading down a dangerous road." Cheap grace was pouring into the church through something he called "new theology."

"Where will it lead?" I inquired.

"There is only one place it can lead," he said, "and that is straight into Babylon!"

Though Jim never went so far as to say the church *was* Babylon, he introduced me to people who would. That happened in 1985 when my wife and I attended a "nonsanctioned" meeting of what our pastor called "offshoots." He, along with other church members, cautioned us not to go. But their warnings only made us more curious. *What do they know?* we thought. *They too have probably been infected by this new theology.*

Still, when we finally heard someone publicly state that the Seventh-day Adventist Church was indeed part of Babylon, it didn't seem to have the right ring in our ears. So we began to study the subject in Ellen White's writings for ourselves. It didn't take long before we realized that the Seventh-day Adventist Church wasn't Babylon. Then, as if God had opened our eyes with a vision-restoring salve, we realized that the "offshoot groups" were the misguided ones. We began to see through their veneer of sanctimonious behavior and realized that they were really "ravenous wolves" in disguise. The hostility they displayed as we shared with them the conclusions of our study on Babylon confirmed our conclusion.

Having gone through this experience, my wife and I naturally felt a burden for those who innocently get caught up in such errors. Whenever given the opportunity, we shared what we had learned. During the early 1990s negative attacks upon the Adventist Church began to increase. All over America disgruntled Adventists began leaving the conference congregations to form so-called home churches. The movement became so well organized that it even broadcast church services right into homes via satellite. Because of what we had already encountered, we recognized the trend's dangers.

My family and I had just moved to Arkansas at the time. In our area an unusually large number of people had joined this movement and left our local congregation to begin one of their own. Having won the confidence of one individual, I received an invitation to give a presentation on what Ellen White had to say about the relationship of individual members with the Adventist Church as a whole. As a result a number of people decided to return to the mainstream organization.

The local Adventist pastor was dumbfounded that my talk had produced such positive reactions. He explained that he had been laboring with the group for years and had not been able to get anywhere with them. Now he wanted to know what I had shared that had motivated people to return to the church. I answered that I had simply related some principles from the Bible and Ellen White's writings that my wife and I had learned from our own experience. The pastor then told me about some people in another part of his district whom he felt could benefit from such information and requested that I prepare a written study. I agreed to do so.

When I finished, the pastor asked if he could send the material to several conference and union leaders for review. I consented, but never in my wildest dreams did I expect what would come of it. Someone forwarded the manuscript to the Review and Herald Publishing Association, and it decided to publish the material in book form. In the fall of 1994 the publishing house released it under the title *The Shaking Among God's People*. Much to my surprise, the book quickly became a denominational best-seller both in North America and abroad.

Since that time my wife, Lisa, and I have continued to study the biblical concept of the shaking. For the most part, that first book considered the topic as it relates to our relationship with God's organized church on earth. But now we see it to be much deeper and broader. The shaking involves primarily our relationship with Christ. What will ultimately decide our outcome through the events ahead is whether or not we have found peace and trust in the promised forgiveness of our Savior, Jesus. This in turn will affect how we relate to our fellow church members, especially when they do wrong. It will equip us with a spirit of compassion and forgiveness, because we will be humbled by the fact that God through His compassion has already forgiven us.

My intent in writing *Surviving the Shaking* is to draw readers into a closer relationship with Christ. This sequel to my first book seeks to present Jesus and His forgiving grace as the central pillar of all that we teach as Seventh-day Adventist Christians. Hopefully it will enable our dependency on Jesus to grow stronger and stronger, until we shall be enabled to withstand the tempest winds of the shaking when it finally hits with all its fury. At that time, when everything that can be shaken will be, we can rest in the assurance that "the root of the righteous cannot be moved" (Prov. 12:3, NKJV).

It is my personal prayer that a closer walk with Jesus be the result for all who read *Surviving the Shaking*.

—Keavin Hayden

Section One

A SHAKING OVER INSPIRATION

Chapter 1

TEACHERS SENT FROM GOD

One of the greatest human interest stories in American history is that of Helen Adams Keller (born Tuscumbia, Alabama, June 27, 1880; died June 1, 1968). Born as a normal baby, at the age of 19 months she developed scarlet fever, which left her blind, deaf, and mute. As Helen grew older her only means of communication with others was through abnormal behavior, such as uncontrollable laughter or violent tantrums. Her parents, soon realizing that they could no longer control her, concluded that they would need to send Helen away. Since no special facilities to deal with such problem cases existed in those days, their only option was the state insane asylum.

The thought of relegating her little girl to the asylum was more than Mrs. Keller could bear, so she begged her husband for a little more time to try to find help. Sometime later the Kellers read about a special school for blind persons called Perkins Institute in Boston, Massachusetts. It seemed only a small hope, because not only was the school far away, but it dealt only with those who were blind. Their little girl was not just blind, but deaf and mute as well. But Mr. Keller wrote to the school to see if there might be any possibility of getting help. To their surprise, the school responded by dispatching a very special teacher to Tuscumbia in an attempt to bring meaning to Helen Keller's life. Her name was Annie Mansfield Sullivan.

One day Helen realized that her mother was leaving the house without her. She sat and waited a long time for her return. Though Helen couldn't hear the loudest noise in the world, she could sense the thud of horses' hooves and the vibrations of carriage wheels. They meant that her mother was coming home. As she felt footsteps crossing the porch she ran to meet her mother. Helen held out her arms and felt herself being scooped up. But they were the arms of a stranger. Annie Sullivan had come to Helen in an attempt to help her, but the girl didn't know this. She felt only the threat of a stranger. So Helen began to resist every effort Miss Sullivan tried to make in her behalf.

One of the things that Annie Sullivan quickly discerned was that because everyone had felt sorry for the child, they had let her have her own way. As Miss Sullivan tried to teach her some degree of self-control, Helen became more violent. She kicked and screamed, pinched and cried. Sometimes she would throw objects across the room or growl fiercely like a wild animal. But Annie persisted, re-straining her with loving firmness and consistently trying to set up some means of communication with the little inhabitant of a dark and scary world. Miss Sullivan used what was called the finger al-phabet. Handing Helen an object with which she was familiar, the teacher would then spell out the name of the object to her by mak-ing the shapes of the letters in her hand. But Helen never associated the name with the object or even realized that the fingering was Miss Sullivan's attempt to communicate with her.

April 5, 1887, began like any other day. After breakfast Annie Sullivan and 6-year-old Helen Keller took a walk together in the garden. As they came to an old pump house, Annie pumped out some water into Helen's hand and quickly wrote in her wet palm W-A-T-E-R. At first Helen began to pull away as usual, but then she stopped. A new expression crossed her face. Annie saw the look and quickly spelled again W-A-T-E-R. Helen began to write back, W-A-T . . . With each movement her face grew brighter, for sud-denly *she knew!* The shapes the stranger had been making in her hand had meaning! Everything in the whole world had a name! And she could learn them all! For the first time Helen realized that life had a purpose.

"Oh, yes, Helen," Annie whispered as she bent down to hug the trembling little girl. But Helen pulled away. It was no time for hugs. Dropping to the ground, she thumped on it hard. Name it! she was demanding. In the next few minutes Helen learned six new words. Then a puzzled look came across her face. Almost sacredly she tapped herself on the head. Annie burst out in tearful laughter, "Yes, dear, there's a name for you, too." Then she took the little learner's hand and solemnly spelled H-E-L-E-N.

Next Helen took hold of Miss Sullivan's arm and patted it. At first Annie thought that perhaps it was the girl's way of saying thank you, but then Helen patted her arm again. "Oh," Annie said, "so you want to know who I am, too." Then she wrote in the inquisitive little girl's hand T-E-A-C-H-E-R.

That spring morning two new people left the pump house. The wild little girl was gone, and so was the stranger. For now that they understood and trusted each other they were destined to accomplish great things in life.

As time passed they began to travel, exploring the world together. Helen attended Perkins Institute, where she learned to read braille. Now a whole new world developed in her mind—the world of literary arts. At 9 years of age Helen let it be known that she not only wanted to communicate with her hands but with her mouth like everyone else. This was nearly unheard-of, but with the aid of a special teacher and painstaking effort on Helen's part, she began to speak her first words audibly.

More and more people began to hear about Helen. Newspaper stories appeared about her. A shipbuilder in Maine named a ship after her. Some of the most important people in the world became her friends. At 12 years of age she received an invitation to the White House to meet President Grover Cleveland. But of all the people she met, none ever meant more to her than Annie Sullivan.

In 1904 she graduated with honors from Radcliffe College. At 24 she became a writer and public speaker, traveling and holding lectures with Annie. Then on October 20, 1936, the most tragic thing that could happen to her took place—her beloved Annie died. Helen had faced pain many times in her life, but nothing like this. Her thoughts traveled back through 50 years to the day Annie Sullivan had walked into her life on that front porch in Tuscumbia, Alabama. "That was the most important day of my life," Helen later wrote. "It was my soul's birthday—the day my teacher came to me."

Helen Keller continued to travel extensively, sharing her story, bringing encouragement to all whose life seemed to have no meaning. President Franklin D. Roosevelt commissioned her to visit despondent soldiers blinded during World War II. She lived until she was 87 years old. Then on June 1, 1968, the world bade farewell to one who had extracted so much meaning out of a life so beset with obstacles.

MODERN-DAY HELENS

In a similar way, we are like Helen Keller when it comes to our spiritual condition—we are "wretched, and miserable, and poor, and blind, and naked" (Rev. 3:17). And God, in an attempt to help us, has dispatched special teachers to help us understand both our condition and how to get out of it. We call those teachers prophets. But though the prophets sought only to help, we, as Helen initially did with Annie Sullivan, often perceived their entrance into our lives as that of strangers who threaten our security. As a result, we end up fighting against them as though they were an enemy. Like Ahab, we see them as "troublers" of our peace (see 1 Kings 18:17).

Since we are blind spiritually, we really don't know what it is like to see spiritually. Therefore, we are often content with our condition because we don't know anything different. It is the main reason people in Scripture rejected the prophets sent to them. They had grown comfortable in their blinded state.

God, knowing our condition, had to find a way to communicate with us. Once we sense that the prophets have come to help and not hurt, to lift us up instead of tearing us down, we will lay our defenses aside and begin to learn what heaven has all the while been desiring to teach us. Then we will advance in spiritual knowledge and growth. Because we now hear His voice, we will without delay open the door and invite Him in (Rev. 3:20).

But in order for this to happen God has to teach us just how this divine method of communication works. Otherwise we cannot fully understand what He is scribbling in our hands. All too often we have misunderstood the nature of divine communication. Nevertheless, it is vital that we learn more about how it works, because "as the end draws near and the work of giving the last warning to the world extends, it becomes more important for those who accept present truth to have a clear understanding of the nature and influence of the *Testimonies,*" "the manner in which they are given, and how they should be regarded" (*Testimonies for the Church,* vol. 5, p. 654).

GOD GIVES US EYES

Satan, the father of darkness, loves to work undetected in the dark—in our ignorance of God. He knows that if God's people have no light or guidance, he can then more easily deceive them. God, on the other hand, provides light to His people through the prophets. "Surely the Lord God will do nothing, but he revealeth his secret unto his servants the prophets" (Amos 3:7). Through the prophets God gives His church "eyes" to see Him and to detect Satan's snares.

It is by His gift of inspiration that the church will defeat our great enemy in the end, and he knows it. Therefore he must do everything within his power to keep God's people from reading and utilizing the knowledge that will magnify Christ and thus spell out his doom. He knows that "where there is no vision, the people perish" (Prov. 29:18). Thus he must somehow find a way, as he did with Samson, to blind the church so that it cannot see how he is trying to destroy it. *This he most successfully accomplishes by removing Jesus and His essential role in the plan of salvation as the central, focal point of inspired writings.* To this purpose he works unceasingly to get the people of God to misuse, despise, or ignore the prophetic gift.

God counsels us to "believe not every spirit, but try the spirits whether they are of God: because many false prophets are gone out into the world" (1 John 4:1). John explains that prophets reveal their validity by how they relate to what Christ's salvational role was when He became human (see 1 John 4:2, 3).

The prophet Isaiah gets a little more specific on testing the origin of messages claiming to come from God. He said: "To the law and to the testimony: if they speak not according to this word, it is because there is no light in them" (Isa. 8:20). Notice the two points that indicate a message's truthfulness:

First, the law. The Bible consistently teaches that the purpose of the law is not to save us, but to point out our sinfulness and our need of something outside our ability to live a good life. That's why Paul, in writing about the righteousness that Jesus worked out in His life and death, stated: "But now the righteousness of God *without the law is manifested, being witnessed by the law and the prophets;* even the righteousness of God which is by faith of Jesus Christ unto all and upon all them that believe" (Rom. 3:21, 22). "For if there had been a law given which could have given life, verily righteousness [salvation] should have been by the law. But the scripture hath concluded all under sin, that the promise by faith of Jesus Christ might be given to them that believe" (Gal. 3:21, 22). So in essence, we must test every message by whether or not it to any degree teaches that one can be saved by means of how well an individual keeps the law. If it does, then Isaiah instructs us to reject that idea or teaching as coming from God. It simply has no light in it.

This brings us to the second testing point—the "testimony." A true prophet carries with them a testimony, or witness, about Christ. As a matter of fact, the truest definition of the "spirit of prophecy" is that it is the "testimony of Jesus" (see Rev. 19:10). Referring to the unique role Jesus plays in the redemption process, the apostle Peter declared: "Neither is there salvation in any other: for there is none other name under heaven given among men, whereby we must be saved" (Acts 4:12). The true testimony must declare that the only means of salvation for anyone is a total dependence on what transpired in the earthly life and death of the Son of God as a substitute for our faulty lives. Those who do not clearly distinguish this truth still wander in darkness. It matters not how much they claim to know what is truth, how charismatic they are, or how popular and well respected they are, "if they speak not according to this word, it is because there is no light in them" (Isa. 8:20). Any message without Christ as its central salvational theme is a message of darkness.

Paul summed up Isaiah's two points when he explained to the Galatians that "the law was our schoolmaster to bring us unto Christ, that we might be justified by faith [by relying on His merits]" (Gal. 3:24). This is our job as well—to combine the law and the gospel without getting the two confused, and then demonstrating to the world how they work together.

Now that we have a better understanding as to what constitutes a truly inspired message, let's take a closer look at how inspiration really works!

Chapter 2

THE MECHANICS OF INSPIRATION

The issue of inspiration—understanding why God gave His message and how we should interpret it—will play a big part in determining who will be shaken out. God is not finished communicating with His people through His wonderful prophetic gift. It could be that He will raise up other prophets before the end. No doubt that would create a stir! But even if we don't get another prophet, we have been told that much new light is yet to be revealed from what has already been given us in the Scriptures (read carefully *Counsels to Writers and Editors,* pp. 33-51).

We must make sure that we have a balanced understanding of how inspiration works, lest we fail to keep pace with the new dimensions of light. History teaches us that those who fail to walk in God's increasing light always end up being shaken out of His advancing armies.

As we saw in our last chapter, Helen—frozen in darkness—was fearful and did not realize that a determined individual was reaching through her darkness in an attempt to release her. The device Annie Sullivan used to bring freedom to Helen was a marvelous demonstration of the golden rule. Her teacher got down on her level by immersing herself in Helen's situation and through touch found a breakthrough in communication.

THE GOLDEN RULE OF INTERPRETATION

Similarly, God knows that the only way to get through to our dark world is to meet us where we are. We have already learned that God's government rests on the golden rule. Infinite wisdom employed this redemptive principle when the "Word became flesh" (John 1:14, NKJV), to be "God with us" (Matt. 1:23) as our substitute in the great plan of salvation. The nature of God communicating through inspired writings follows a similar pattern.

Thus the first key in unlocking the Scriptures is to recognize that the Bible is based on the golden rule and that we must interpret it through this principle. Ellen White definitely recognized this golden rule concept in the Incarnation as being the model for the inspired writings as well. She said that "the Bible, with its God-given truths expressed in the language of men, presents a union of the divine and human. Such a union existed in the nature of Christ, who was the Son of God and the Son of man. Thus it is true of the Bible, as it was of Christ, that 'the Word was made flesh, and dwelt among us.' John 1:14" (*The Great Controversy,* p. vi). "The Bible is not given to us in grand superhuman language. Jesus, in order to reach man where he is, took humanity. The Bible must be given in the language of men. Everything that is human is imperfect. Different meanings are expressed by the same word; there is not one word for each distinct idea. The Bible was given for practical purposes" (*Selected Messages,* book 1, p. 20).

Throughout history God has sought to communicate His will to the world in the language of the time. For this reason the Bible is a record that we must view in the context of time, place, and people. Only by reconstructing the cultural setting in which God spoke can we realize the message of truth He conveyed. The golden rule, then, is the first rule of interpretation and must be our primary guide as we walk through the Bible, especially as we seek to translate those messages to our own time.

This golden rule principle of interpretation is practical in nature. It deals with real-life circumstances in the context of the time and place in which they occurred. The concept's greatest faculty is common sense. In other words, it has an "all things considered" mindset. I think it is what Ellen White meant when she said that God gave the Bible for "practical purposes."

Another major universal principle that we must keep in mind is the weblike nature of inspiration. Paul expressed this dynamic in 1 Corinthians 14:32, in which he stated that even "the spirits of the prophets are subject to the prophets." They speak out of their own experience and background and thus to a great extent control and shape what they speak for God. And a vital part of that experience and background is the rest of Scripture. The words of the Bible are integrated with each other, commenting on and expanding earlier revelation. "The Bible is its own expositor. Scripture is to be compared with scripture. The student should learn to view the word as a whole, and see the relation of its parts" (*Education,* p. 190). "The plan of redemption is comprehensive; but its parts are few, and each part depends on the others, while all work together with the utmost simplicity and in entire harmony" (*The Watchman,* Nov. 28, 1905).

It is essential that we employ common sense to put separate but related truths together if we ever hope to clearly understand what God is trying to say to us. People often focus on and magnify one piece of the puzzle that in no way represents the overall picture of truth. Failure to recognize these imperative principles of inspiration has shipwrecked many a spiritual pilgrim by leading them to distorted conclusions that don't fit the general tenor of the inspired writings as a whole.

VERBAL VERSUS THOUGHT INSPIRATION

Contrary to the beliefs of a large segment of Christianity, the testimonies of the prophets come to us not through verbal inspiration, but rather as inspired thoughts. The words chosen by the prophets are not what is inspired, but the ideas that the words are attempting to convey is what the prophet received through divine revelation. We always get into trouble when we take just a few words written by the prophet and try to form our conclusions only around them. Rather, we should collect all that we can on any given topic and seek the bigger idea behind those words. The words, in and of themselves, are an imperfect vehicle that seeks to present more perfect principles and ideas. "The Lord speaks to human beings in imperfect speech, in order that the degenerate senses, the dull, earthly perception, of earthly beings may comprehend His words. . . . The Bible, perfect as it is in its simplicity, does not answer to the great ideas of God; for infinite ideas cannot be perfectly embodied in finite vehicles of thought" (*Selected Messages,* book 1, p. 22).

Although my car may be imperfect in that it has worn shocks, dented fenders, and a cracked windshield, it can still get me where I need to go. So it is with biblical revelation. Though it must work within the confines of imperfect human expression, it still manages to present the information necessary to get to the eternal world if people so desire.

An example of why the view of verbal inspiration is not reliable is Jesus' story of the rich man and Lazarus. If taken literally and at face value, then we have strong evidence in favor of the immortality of the soul. But in commenting on this parable Ellen White exemplifies the baseline principle, which the Lord Himself used, regarding how inspiration works. "In this parable Christ was meeting the people on their own ground. The doctrine of a conscious state of existence between death and the resurrection was held by many of those who were listening to Christ's words. The Saviour knew of their ideas, and He framed His parable so as to inculcate important truths through these preconceived opinions. . . . *He used the prevailing opinion to convey the idea He wished to make prominent to all"* (*Christ's Object Lessons,* p. 263; italics supplied).

Here we have an object lesson as to how inspiration really works. Jesus, the perfect and divine source of truth, used imperfect and even erroneous human opinions to convey vital concepts of heavenly origin. The inspired teachings of the prophets often employed the same approach.

THINGS HARD TO UNDERSTAND

Yet some get frustrated when they discover that inspired counsel, whether it be the Bible or the writings of Ellen White, is not always as cut and dried as they would like. Inspired writings may have seeming contradictions that we may never completely understand in this life. "For now we see through a glass, darkly [in a riddle]; but then face to face: *now I know in part;* but then shall I know even as also I am known" (1 Cor. 13:12; brackets taken from King James marginal reading; see also verses 8-10). Inspiration always comes to us in bits and pieces. It is for us, with the aid of the Holy Spirit, to put the puzzle together—line upon line, precept upon precept, here a little and there a little—until we get the bigger picture. And even when we get that bigger idea, it will still be a relatively imperfect photograph of the absoluteness of God's beautiful character and divine plan.

God designed this both to keep us dependent on Him and to help us learn to reason things out for ourselves. It prevents us from feeling comfortable with, and leaning to, our own understanding. And it better prepares us to work out problems and situations not directly addressed in Scripture. But sad to say, when many discover seemingly inconsistent teachings by the prophets, they give up their faith in the inspired writings altogether. The apostle Peter once commented: "Even as our beloved brother Paul also according to the wisdom given unto him hath written unto you; as also in all his epistles, speaking in them of these things; in which are some things hard to be understood, which they that are unlearned and unstable wrest, as they do also the other scriptures, unto their own destruction" (2 Peter 3:15, 16).

With a clearer concept of how biblical inspiration works, in our next two chapters we shall examine Ellen White's role as a latter-day prophet and just how her writings relate to the revelation of Jesus Christ in His Word, the Bible.

Chapter 3

HAD YE BELIEVED MOSES

It must have been an exasperating day for Jesus. He had come to our world to bring healing and salvation. Yet every time He did His work of physical healing, evidence of His divine power to heal spiritually as well, many of His own people condemned Him.

One Sabbath Jesus strolled by the Pool of Bethesda and healed a man who had suffered for 38 years. When the religious leadership found out that Jesus had healed the man, they publicly condemned Him for violating the Sabbath, and for claiming equality with God. Jesus seized the opportunity to teach an important lesson about the ultimate purpose of the prophetic gift. He knew that their failure to understand the real intent of the prophetic messages was keeping them from accepting Him as their Messiah.

John 5:15-47 records the incident. We should study this portion of Scripture carefully, for its message is as significant to Seventh-day Adventists living today as it was for God's people of that time.

In verses 19-30 Jesus presents the truth that the Father had appointed Him as the way of salvation and that anyone who believed this fact "has hold of eternal life, and does not come up for judgement, but has already passed from death to life" (verse 24, NEB). Then Jesus proceeded to say that it was not just His own declaration about His Messiahship that God had given to them for evidence. "If I testify on my own behalf, that testimony does not hold good. There is another who bears witness for me, and I know his testimony holds. Your messengers have been sent to John [the Baptist]; you have his testimony to the truth. Not that I rely on human testimony, but I remind you of it for your own salvation. John was a lamp, burning brightly, and for a time you were ready to exult in his light. But I rely on a testimony higher than John's. There is enough to testify that the Father has sent me, in the works my Father gave me to do and finish—the very works I have in hand [in other words, the issue under discussion of My healing the crippled man]. This testimony to me was given by the Father who sent me, although you never heard his voice, or saw his form. But his word has found no home in you, for you do not believe the one whom he sent" (verses 31-38, NEB).

Then Jesus honed in on His point. "You study the scriptures diligently, supposing that in having them you have eternal life; yet, although their testimony points to me, you refuse to come to me for that life. . . . Do not imagine that I shall be your accuser at the Father's tribunal. Your accuser is Moses, the very Moses on whom you have set your hope. If you believed Moses you would believe what I tell you, *for it was about me that he wrote.* But if you do not believe what he wrote, how are you to believe what I say?" (verses 39-47, NEB).

THE SHADOW OR THE SUBSTANCE?

In my opinion this story contains the most important lesson Scripture has to teach us. Inspired writings are not the source of eternal life—Jesus Christ is. The testimonies of the prophets are merely designed to point this fact out to us. The Scriptures, in and of themselves, can do nothing to save us. But they can lead us to salvation by giving us an understanding of the unique role Jesus plays in the plan of salvation.

Christ not only brings us salvation; He *is* our salvation! Whether or not we are saved in the end will not be determined by how good or bad a life record we have. It will not result because we have publicly acknowledged someone as a true prophet. Rather, it will depend on whether or not we accept the perfect life and atoning death of Jesus Christ as being adequate to clear us in the judgment.

Once we grasp this point, then the Scriptures come alive with the drama of how earnestly Jesus—and the prophets who testified of His unique salvational role—tried to get people to see and acknowledge this fact. Being the wise teacher that He is, God provided object lesson after object lesson to help His ancient people see it. But in their blindness of heart they always ended up being content to settle into the shadow rather than moving forward to grasp the substance. The visible demonstration of the lessons absorbed their interest more than the invisible truth they taught (see 2 Cor. 4:18).

For example, God provided Israel with an earthly demonstration of how the plan of salvation works by giving them the Hebrew tabernacle services. The ceremonies focused on the all-important role that the second member of the Godhead, Jesus Christ, would play in saving them. Yet for the most part, generation after generation missed the point, because they focused on the ceremonies instead of the lessons they taught. Amazingly, they passed over the Passover (see 1 Cor. 5:7). By the time the substance appeared in the person of the true Lamb of God, the leaders of His people were ready to do away with Him through crucifixion and continue their offerings of bulls and goats (see Heb. 9).

Another example is God's law. Writing to the Romans, Paul stated that "I had not known sin, but by the law" (Rom. 7:7). The major purpose of the law was to point out our sinfulness and our need of a Savior outside ourselves. Only one person in the entire universe qualifies to be that Savior. It is not some canonized saint, reincarnated guru, or even a Seventh-day Adventist who believes he or she can reach a state of perfect, spiritual existence through lawkeeping and obedience, but Jesus Christ alone!

Israel had so focused on obeying the law that they missed Christ, the one whom the schoolmaster (the law) was trying to lead them to. That is why they were in such a hurry that crucifixion Friday to kill the Lord of the Sabbath. They needed to make sure they were home in time to avoid breaking the Sabbath commandment. Their observance of the law was of more importance to them than their total reliance on the substitutionary record of the only One who could keep the law perfectly in their behalf.

And last, Jesus pointed out that if they were lost, it wouldn't be because He condemned them in the judgment. He said it would be Moses, the one whom they claimed to trust, who would stand as their accuser. And why? Because in fulfilling his role as a true prophet, Moses had sought to prepare them to accept Jesus as the Messiah—"for it was about me that he [Moses] wrote" (John 5:46, NEB). But because they rejected the substance of the prophetic writings (Jesus), they clung to the shadow (Moses) as though he could save them. That's why they stated to another man whom Jesus healed: "We are disciples of Moses. We know that God spoke to Moses, but as for this fellow [Jesus], we do not know where he comes from" (John 9:28, 29, NEB).

WHERE DO WE STAND?

It is here that we must honestly confront ourselves with a most crucial question: Are we as Seventh-day Adventists in danger of making the same mistake as did God's people in the past by relying more upon shadows than the substance of Christ? Sadly, our own church history reveals that we are not only in danger of making the same mistake, but we have actually done so.

For example, consider our historical approach toward God's law. Back in the early days of our church we were known far and wide for our expositions on its binding claims. Everywhere our pioneers went they carried with them a chart of the Ten Commandments. Did you ever examine one of those old charts they used? It would begin: "I am the Lord thy God. . . . Thou shalt have no other gods before me." Notice the ellipses here. We use ellipses to skip over words we consider irrelevant so as to get more quickly to the important stuff.

Now turn to Exodus 20 and take a look at what the charts regarded as not significant. Verses 2 and 3 read: "I am the Lord thy God, *which have brought thee out of the land of Egypt, out of the house of bondage.* Thou shalt have no other gods before me." Do you see it? It was none other than Jesus who was telling them that He had personally delivered them "out of the house of bondage." In other words, He set them free by His mighty works. This is nothing more, nothing less, than an Old Testament message of liberating justification! Before God ever asks us to attempt to obey His law, He assures us that we have already been accepted as though we have perfectly performed that obedience. Obedience without such assurance is still bondage. It is not our obedience, but our acceptance of Christ's obedience—along with His death—that fulfills the highest demands of the law and sets us free.

Our early pioneers' fascination for divine law without Christ—the shadow instead of the substance—led our church to that fateful, historical General Conference session of 1888 in Minneapolis, Minnesota. At those meetings Ellet J. Waggoner, Alonzo T. Jones, Ellen White, and others tried to impress our church leaders with the fact that Jesus had been taking a back seat in our biblical presentations. Because of the resistance those messages received, Ellen White declared that we as a people were in the process of repeating the history of the Jews (see *Review and Herald,* Mar. 18, 1890).

SOMEBODY MUST DECREASE

Now we come to what is perhaps the most touchy issue among Seventh-day Adventists—how we relate to the ministry of Ellen G. White. Was she shadow—or substance? Can we be saved just because we believe she received the prophetic gift from God? What was the real purpose of her ministry and just how should we regard her writings?

As we answer such sensitive questions let's begin by reviewing the ministry of John the Baptist. Jesus Himself stated that there had never been a prophet greater than John (Matt. 11:11). All the other prophets could declare Christ's Messiahship only through symbolism, but John pointed out Jesus, the "Lamb of God" and Savior of the world, in the flesh (John 1:29). Earlier we read how Jesus noted to His audience that John had testified about Him (John 5:32, 33). But even the Baptist's own disciples became confused as his shadow gave way to the substance of Christ.

In the early days of his ministry John himself had been the focal point of the people's interest. But when Jesus' ministry began, John's popularity dwindled. More and more people began to focus on Jesus, causing grave concern among some of the Baptist's disciples. They approached him about it. His response clearly demonstrated that he recognized what was happening (John 3:26-36). The heart of his testimony that day appears in his statement that "he must increase, but I must decrease" (verse 30).

Ellen White observes that "he [John] saw the tide of popularity turning away from himself to the Saviour. Day by day the crowds about him lessened. When Jesus came from Jerusalem to the region about Jordan, the people flocked to hear Him. The number of His disciples increased daily. . . . But the disciples of John looked with jealousy upon the growing popularity of Jesus" (*The Desire of Ages,* p. 178).

In contrast to the blindness of his own disciples, the Baptist recognized the unique role that Jesus would play. "So John had been called to direct the people to Jesus, and it was his joy to witness the success of the Saviour's work. He said, 'This my joy therefore is fulfilled. He must increase, but I must decrease.' Looking in faith to the Redeemer, John had risen to the height of self-abnegation. He sought not to attract men to himself, but to lift their thoughts higher and still higher, until they should rest upon the Lamb of God. He himself had been only a voice, a cry in the wilderness. Now with joy he accepted silence and obscurity, that the eyes of all might be turned to the Light of life" (*ibid.,* p. 179).

Ellen White saw John's example as a precedent for everyone called to a ministry for Christ—even her own.

THE LESSER LIGHT

To answer our questions regarding the prophetic purpose of Ellen White, we must first deal with another question: Do Seventh-day Adventists place the writings of Ellen White above, or on a plane equal with, the Bible, the Word of God? If not, then exactly what relationship do they have with the Scriptures?

The answer to this is really quite simple. No, the church does not regard Ellen White's writings equal with the Scriptures. Nor did Ellen White.

- "The Spirit was not given—nor can it ever be bestowed—to supersede the Bible; for the Scriptures explicitly state that the Word of God is the standard by which all teaching and experience must be tested" (*The Great Controversy,* p. vii).

- "The written testimonies are not to give new light, but to impress vividly upon the heart the truths of inspiration already revealed [in the Bible]" (*Testimonies for the Church,* vol. 2, p. 605).

- "Brother J would confuse the mind by seeking to make it appear that the light God has given through the *Testimonies* is an addition to the Word of God, but in this he presents the matter in a false light" (*ibid.,* vol. 5, p. 663).

Ellen White regarded the Scriptures as a sacred, one-of-a-kind book containing the ultimate revelation and testimony of Jesus Christ for us living today. Unlike John, she could not point us to Jesus in His tangible, physical flesh. But her ministry bears record that she did the next best thing—she directed us to Jesus in the Word of God, the Bible.

Her husband, James White, also made clear what he believed was the proper role of the prophetic gift bestowed upon his wife. "God in much mercy has pitied the weakness of His people, and has set the gifts in the gospel church to correct our errors, and lead us to His living Word [the Bible]" (*Review and Herald,* Apr. 21, 1851). "Every Christian is therefore in duty bound to take the Bible as a perfect rule of faith and duty. He should pray fervently to be aided by the Holy Spirit in searching the Scriptures for the whole truth, and for his whole duty. *He is not at liberty to turn from them [the Scriptures] to learn his duty through any of the gifts. We say that the very moment he does, he places the gifts in a wrong place, and takes an extremely dangerous position.* The Word [the Bible] should be in front, and the eye of the church should be placed upon it, as the rule to walk by, and the fountain of wisdom, from which to learn duty in 'all good works.' But if a portion of the church err from the truths of the Bible, and become weak, and sickly, and the flock become scattered, so that it seems necessary for God to employ the gifts of the Spirit to correct, revive and heal the erring, we should let Him work" (*Review and Herald,* Oct. 3, 1854; italics supplied).

Though many treat her as such, Ellen White never intended for her work to be a substitute for, or addition to, the Bible. Her writings were never designed to do our thinking for us, but to help teach us how to think for ourselves in the biblical context. Contrary to what many Adventists today assume, Ellen White never considered what she wrote as final authority. Instead, she always pointed to the Scriptures as the only "authoritative and infallible revelation of [God's] will" (*The Great Controversy,* p. vii).

"In public labor do not make prominent and quote that which Sister White has written, as authority to sustain your positions. To do this will not increase faith in the testimonies. Bring your evidences, clear and plain, from the Word of God. A 'Thus saith the Lord' is the strongest testimony you can possibly present to the people" (*Selected Messages,* book 3, pp. 29, 30).

Referring to the Bible and the Christ revealed in it, Ellen White said that her testimonies were "a lesser light to lead to the greater light" (*Colporteur Ministry,* p. 125). What was she trying to tell us through this metaphor? Did she mean that her writings were not divinely inspired? Let me share an example on this point.

When I was a young boy, I had in my bedroom a light switch that glowed in the dark. With this handy aid I could get out of my bed when it was completely dark, walk straight to that lighted switch, and turn on the ceiling light that then illuminated the entire room. That lesser light, when used, always provided me with greater light. It saved me from having to grope along the walls, bruising my legs and stubbing my toes, while looking for the light switch. Was it valuable to me? Of course. And so is the gift of prophecy through Ellen White. If rightly employed, it will illuminate our darkened understandings with vital insights into biblical teachings.

However, once I turned on my ceiling light my wall switch became less prominent. It had served its purpose, and now I became less dependent upon it. Likewise, Ellen White's writings illuminate our pathway until we can clearly delineate the biblical role that Christ plays in the plan of salvation. Once our minds grasp Jesus in that biblical context, we discover that the real power is in the Word! Then, just as John the Baptist's role decreased once he had accomplished his task of making the Messiah known, so Ellen White's role will take on a less prominent position in the experience of Adventists who have through her found Jesus in the Scriptures. Once you have discovered this Pearl of great price (Jesus), you have found the ultimate truth to which all other truths are subordinate.

Now, I know that many will regard any suggestion of Ellen White becoming less prominent as heresy. They will charge that it is the first step toward rejecting her writings. But the truth is that many Adventists base their faith upon a "thus saith Sister White." Just as the Jews said, "We have Abraham, and we have Moses," some Adventists, by the way they often reason, unwittingly declare, "We have Ellen White." When they examine their spiritual status, they check to see if they are living up to all the counsels that Ellen White gave instead of determining whether or not they have total assurance of salvation based on their faith in what Jesus did for them.

When we use Ellen White's writings as a replacement for the Word of God, when we use her counsels on diet or dress or any other aspect of human behavior as a means to make us holy or right with God, be assured that her writings no longer fulfill their divinely appointed role. The devil instead uses them to weaken the church and its members. Such a crippling effect is evident when: (1) the study of Ellen White's literature lessens the time we spend in the Word of God and we can quote more of her material than we can the Bible; and (2) we find our ability to witness to those outside our faith limited because we can prove what we believe only from one of Ellen White's books. If people want to call this heresy, then so be it! But I believe with all my heart that if Ellen White were living today she would say the same thing, because she said it back in her lifetime.

Speaking to a group at the Battle Creek College library in 1901, she urged them, "Lay Sister White to one side. Do not quote my words again as long as you live until you can obey the Bible. When you make the Bible your food, your meat and your drink, when you make its principles the elements of your character, you will know better how to receive counsel from God. I exalt the precious Word before you today. Do not repeat what I have said, saying, 'Sister White said this,' and 'Sister White said that.' Find out what the Lord God of Israel says, and then do what He commands" (MS 43, 1901).

In 1906 Dr. David Paulson wrote to Mrs. White, stating, "I was led to conclude and most firmly believe that every word that you ever spoke in public or private, that every letter you wrote under any and all circumstances, was as inspired as the Ten Commandments. I held that view with absolute tenacity against innumerable objections raised to it by many who were occupying prominent positions in the cause." He then asked her if he should continue his position.

Her reply shocked him, as it does many in our church today who are zealous to make Ellen White's authority supreme. She told him: "My brother, you have studied my writings diligently, and you have never found that I have made any such claims, neither will you find that the pioneers in our cause made such claims" (letter 206, 1906). History has proved again and again that those who take extreme views toward Ellen White's writings—making more out of them than she intended—eventually lose confidence in them when confronted with things in them that they cannot immediately explain.

It often appears that those who use Ellen White's writings in an extreme way (relying on her more than on the Bible) are her defenders. But the reality is that they are the very ones who bring the greatest reproach upon the prophetic gift. It is those who use her as a stepping-stone to Christ in the Scriptures who really comprehend what God intended when He gave the prophetic gift to our church.

DELIGHTING IN THE LIGHT

Does this mean then that Ellen White received her counsel from an inferior source than that of the Bible writers? Were her writings less inspired? Many Adventists today stress, as did Luther, the concept of *sola scriptura*, meaning that the Bible alone is to be our only rule of faith. And that is true. We do not need Ellen White's writings to prove the biblical points of faith we hold in common as a people. We can substantiate all of our beliefs by the Word of God alone.

But many go overboard with *sola scriptura* by arguing that if we just study our Bibles well enough we don't need the gift of prophecy. While it is true we do not need these additional revelations of the Spirit to prove the points of our biblical faith, the remnant church will be in constant danger if it ignores them. They have been a means of keeping the remnant church on track since its inception, and will continue to aid in guiding it into the kingdom by ever pointing to its power source—Jesus as revealed in His Word.

And here a question arises. Why don't people feel the need of these latter-day revelations of the Spirit? We often attribute it to rebellion and obstinacy, but there might be other reasons for their aversion to God's potent magnifier of the Word.

People have often misused, misunderstood, and even abused the writings of Ellen White. Such abuse has made her writings seem narrow and even unreasonable. Some have presented them as focusing on rigid rules and not with people in a personal, warm, and caring way. We fight over her counsel when we could delight in the light. Such conflict has generated negative feelings toward something God gave us for our own protection and encouragement. Her writings are to be our "meat in due season," the manna of our minds, because Christ, the bread of life, is their central interest and reference. But instead of being a telescope to behold Christ and His beautiful plan of salvation, they have often become a microscope to investigate the errors of fellow believers. The shame of it is that Jesus gets lost in the process.

We must ever remember that the gift of prophecy is the testimony of Jesus. God has provided its mighty and timely counsels in order to open our eyes to the salvation that Christ offers us, just as the Perkins Institute sent Annie Sullivan to open Helen's eyes to the unknown world around her. Such counsels are God's chosen method to bring us closer to Him. He seeks to make them very personal. Never should they be forced upon us by others. If we can deal with the ways in which people are abusing them, it will free them to do their healing, graceful ministry as Christ originally intended. And like Helen, we will be awakened to a new world of ideas about Him. Yes, they are to lead us to Christ in His Word. When that is accomplished, their purpose will be fulfilled.

Those among us who fail to comprehend the salvational role of Christ through this prophetic gift are on shaky ground. Like Korah and his camp, their faith in the organized movement and the prophet that God appointed to lead it will give way when the shaking comes.

Chapter 4

THE ROLE OF ELLEN WHITE

We can only imagine what the early Adventist pioneers must have thought when young Ellen Harmon began having visions that she claimed were from God. Since they lived in an age that expected women to be seen and not heard, they were no doubt at first skeptical. After all, many others had made similar claims to divine revelation.

Yet some tested all things by the Word of God. Their investigation of Joel 2:28-32 revealed to them the fact that God had promised in the last days to restore the prophetic gift to His people. Other Bible passages, such as Ephesians 4, taught them that Christ would indeed provide the prophetic gift until the Christian church actually achieved a mature faith and unified relationship with Christ and with each other. Such Bible texts, her dramatic conversion and focus on Jesus, their firsthand observations of Ellen White while in vision, and the truthfulness of her messages all led them to conclude that God was fulfilling His promise to the remnant as foretold in Joel 2:32. They realized that the remnant spoken of in Joel 2 was the same one that the devil was furious with in Revelation 12:17, because it cradled that same holy Child that the apostolic church had lauded to the world.

Since those early days that prophetic gift has indeed incurred much opposition and criticism from both within and without the church. Yet it has been the very means by which God has established, built up, guided, and preserved His remnant, ever seeking to focus it on Christ and His ministry. Though the church still widely accepts Ellen White's writings, many misconceptions and much misinformation have clouded their real purpose and primary focus. Naturally this confuses church members as to how they should relate to them. Such misunderstanding breeds animosity toward the writings. It is upon this point that Satan will make his last-ditch efforts to attack the Adventist Church from within.

OBJECT OF THE TESTIMONIES

The Bible declares that God is love (1 John 4:8). If that is so, then all things that come from Him do so in the context of that love. However, many times we fail to understand the loving nature of the prophetic gift.

Recognizing that our primary problem is unbelief in God's credibility, Paul in 2 Timothy 3:15 tells us that the main object of the Scriptures is to make us "wise unto salvation through faith . . . in Jesus Christ." Actually "the whole Bible is a manifestation of Christ" (*Signs of the Times,* Feb. 3, 1904). What inspiration really boils down to is selling us on God. The Bible's main thrust is to convince us about Him as a person. It shows us the way He relates to His sinful children and reveals the plan He has ingeniously forged to reinstate us into His eternal family. Once we grasp what it has to say about God, it will enable us to commune with Him through His Word.

After having inspired us about the kind of person God is, Paul affirms the Bible as the greatest "how to" book our world will ever see. Its doctrines, reproofs, corrections, and instructions, as exhibited in law, history, and prophecy, will help us to do right until we are "thoroughly furnished unto all good works" (2 Tim. 3:17).

The Spirit of Prophecy, as found in the writings of Ellen White, follows this same formula. (Note: We often refer to Ellen White's writings as the Spirit of Prophecy. Technically, the term can apply to all prophetic writings and specifically designates the Holy Spirit who inspired them.) The Spirit of Prophecy is first and primarily the "testimony of Jesus," His person and His work. Then it is His wonderful insights on how to thrive successfully in a practical relationship with Him in a more modern context. Such vital instruction becomes "flesh" for us today (see John 6:47-58). This "truth as it is in Jesus" is always positively refreshing, as it causes us to place the burden of our salvation on what Christ has done for us. It fills us with vibrant love for God that spills over in creative, saving sympathy for our fellow human beings.

A wonderful chapter in volume 5 of *Testimonies for the Church* entitled "The Nature and Influence of the 'Testimonies'" teaches about this creative influence of the inspired counsels (pp. 654-691). It offers insight as to how to make the Testimonies valuable in our lives. Reading this chapter will go a long way in helping us to discern God's purpose in giving these last-day testimonies of His Spirit.

Following is a brief list of some other specific reasons God sent the Testimonies and what He hopes to accomplish through them:

- Awaken sinners to duty (*Testimonies for the Church,* vol. 5, p. 667)
- Bring God's people into unity (*ibid.,* vol. 3, pp. 360, 361)
- Bring people back to the neglected Word of God (*ibid.,* vol. 5, p. 665)
- Simplify great truths already given in God's Word (*ibid.,* vol. 2, p. 605)
- Prepare people to stand in the last days (*Selected Messages,* book 1, pp. 41, 42, 45)
- Separate sin from God's people (*Testimonies for the Church,* vol. 5, p. 662)
- Warn, counsel, reprove, comfort, and encourage God's people (*ibid.,* p. 665)
- Instruct concerning His will (*ibid.,* p. 661)
- Perfect holiness in God's people (*ibid.,* vol. 2, pp. 452, 453)
- Point out defects of character (*ibid.,* vol. 5, pp. 234, 674)
- Correct those who err from Bible truth (*Early Writings,* p. 78)
- Separate wrongdoers from God's people (*Testimonies for the Church,* vol. 3, p. 324)
- Show backsliders and sinners their true condition (*ibid.,* vol. 2, p. 608)

• Safeguard God's people against delusions (*Selected Messages,* book 1, pp. 31, 48)

Are these not all worthy endeavors calculated to bring us both present and eternal good by ultimately leading us to place total trust in Jesus Christ? Do they not come to us out of love? Yet Satan does his very best to unsettle our faith in God by creating doubt in us concerning the very counsel that He has sent to help us (see *Selected Messages,* book 1, p. 48; book 2, p. 78).

Because their surgical nature oftentimes touches the nerve of something we cherish in our heart, we are more inclined to yield our confidence in the divine gift than to abandon our indulgences. Thus many find some fault with Ellen White and her writings. Though some claim salvation by grace, and consequently argue that Ellen White doesn't teach it, they are still enslaved to a legalistic mind-set. It is because their hope is still riveted in their performance that they struggle with anything that points out imperfections in them. They do not understand how inspiration works. Therefore they end up rebelling against their schoolmaster, whose discipline God intended only to point them to Christ.

MAKING OF GOOD EFFECT

Again, all of this comes into focus when we understand that the ultimate purpose and object of the Spirit of Prophecy is to reveal Jesus to us. It is in actuality the "testimony" of Him (see Rev. 1:2; 12:17; 19:10). It is natural for us to get a short-sighted view of the prophets when we read inspired writings. We tend to regard them as authority figures presenting lists of "do's" and "don'ts." But when we focus solely on the "do's" and "don'ts," the devil uses the light switch of the prophetic gift to turn the lights out on God's character. By making God appear as one who is simply looking for arbitrary human sacrifices—things that we must give up or else—Satan eclipses His character. Though the sacrifice of things will in many cases be necessary for our own good, that is not what God wants us to focus on when we study the inspired writings.

Because of our unique purpose as God's remnant people called to proclaim God's downtrodden law—and specifically the

Sabbath—we have tended to be oriented toward the "letter of the law." It has made us prone to both Laodicea's legalism and spiritual lethargy. As a result, God sent us a message that we should "of all professing Christians . . . be foremost in uplifting Christ before the world" (*Gospel Workers,* p. 156).

In 1888 the church did not understand this message and emphasis. Consequently, we resisted it because we perceived it as a threat to our unique mission as defenders of God's law. Such a reaction made the writings of Ellen White—and our use of the Bible as well—of "none effect." It was in this context that Ellen White wrote that the devil's last deception would be to make the Spirit of Prophecy of none effect (see *Selected Messages,* book 1, p. 48). The statement appeared in a letter she sent to Uriah Smith, the editor of the *Review and Herald.* In his desire to keep Adventists focused on the law, Smith had resisted the message of Christ's grace. His attempt to use certain Ellen White statements to that end is what prompted her letter of warning and reproof regarding the misuse of her testimonies.

The resulting debate over the law caused many leaders to lose sight of Jesus and His testimony. So it is today. Satan doesn't care what the remnant believers haggle over—be it women's role in ministry, what type of music is appropriate in the worship, lifestyle issues such as dress and diet, or the interpretation of certain prophecies—as long as he can keep their eyes diverted from who Jesus is and what He is really like. The devil succeeds in destroying individuals despite the fact that they have great truth sitting in their backyard. This is not to imply that the church will not have to iron out some of these issues, but simply a reminder that we must not lose sight of Jesus and the way He applied the golden rule to others in the process.

During the 1888 controversy the denomination's hardline portrayal of God through the law had made Him appear as one whose only concern toward us was "thou shalt" and "thou shalt not." The righteousness by faith message, which Ellen White solidly endorsed, sought to reveal His character as an expression of love. Even today, if truly understood, this message will clear up our false concepts about our heavenly Father.

"But," you might say, "where should we go to find the truth

about what was presented in 1888?" To me the most simple, pristine declaration of the righteousness by faith message, outside the writings of the apostle Paul and Martin Luther, appears in Ellen White's presentation on the subject, the book *Steps to Christ*. If we read it with an open heart and mind, we cannot help falling in love with God.

It all relates back to the difference between how converted and unconverted individuals perceive Him. After all, true conversion really constitutes an attitude change toward God. "The unconverted man thinks of God as unloving, as severe, and even revengeful; His presence is thought to be a constant restraint, His character an expression of 'Thou shalt not.' His service is regarded as full of gloom and hard requirements. But when Jesus is seen upon the cross, as the gift of God because He loved man, the eyes are opened to see things in a new light. God as revealed in Christ is not a severe judge, an avenging tyrant, but a merciful and loving Father. . . . There is nothing that more decidedly distinguishes the Christian from the worldly man than the estimate he has of God [what he perceives God to be like]" (*Selected Messages,* book 1, pp. 183, 184).

POSITIVE EFFECTS

When rightly used, Ellen White's writings have always had positive effects as they give their readers a right perspective on God, thus leading them to a higher plane of Christian experience. It is this point—that of what fruit her writings have produced—that should be the deciding evidence of whether or not those writings are divinely inspired. Never should we judge her on the basis of infallibility.

The positive effect her writings have had upon their readers has been a subject of comment among both Adventists and non-Adventists alike. News commentator Paul Harvey stated in his September 25, 1997, broadcast: "Women have been honored on American postage stamps for more than 100 years, starting with one woman who was not an American, Queen Isabella in 1893. Since then, 86 women have been honored ranging from Martha Washington to Marilyn Monroe; also many women authors like Louisa May Alcott, Emily Dickinson, Willa Cather, and Rachael Carson.

"But I can name an American woman author who has never

been honored thus, though her writings have been translated into 148 languages. More than Marx or Tolstoy, more than Agatha Christie, more than William Shakespeare. Only now is the world coming to appreciate her recommended prescription for optimum spiritual and physical health: Ellen White! Ellen White? You don't know her? Get to know her."

Several years ago the Institute of Church Ministry at Andrews University conducted a study that compared the Christian attitude and behavior of Seventh-day Adventists who read her books on a regular basis with those who do not. The study concluded: "Readers have a closer relationship with Christ, more certainty of their standing with God, and are more likely to have identified their spiritual gifts. They are more in favor of spending for public evangelism and contribute more heavily to local missionary projects. They feel more prepared for witnessing and actually engage in more witnessing and outreach programs. They are more likely to study the Bible daily, to pray for specific people, to meet in fellowship groups, and to have daily family worship. They see their church more positively. They are responsible for winning more converts" (*Seventh-day Adventists Believe* . . . , p. 227).

Who wouldn't want such results in their lives? While we may appreciate human literary works—their theories and teachings—let's not place our trust there. We have the privilege of going straight to the Bible and the testimonies of Ellen White. When we start using these heavenly gifts as God intended, then we may have complete assurance that we will have right results.

As we by faith "believe his prophets," we will surely "prosper" in that they will cause us to fall in love with Jesus. This will ultimately "establish" us in the gift of salvation (see 2 Chron. 20:20). "And this is life eternal, that they might know thee the only true God, and Jesus Christ, whom thou hast sent" (John 17:3). Then as God looks down upon the righteous impact His prophetic gift is having upon His people, He will be satisfied that the divine purpose of His communication has been fulfilled. Thus will His people be "rooted and built up in him [Christ], and stablished in the faith" (Col. 2:7). By this means they will be able to "stand fast in the Lord" when the shaking time comes (Phil. 4:1).

Section Two

A SHAKING OVER THEOLOGY

Chapter 5

SALVATION IS CLOSER THAN YOU THINK

God has commissioned Seventh-day Adventists to present to the world a balanced view of how the law and the gospel fit together in the plan of salvation. To confuse the two will mar our ability to carry out our appointed task successfully. It will also make us more susceptible to being shaken out of the Advent movement. This chapter seeks to help us sort out these things in our own personal experience, thus better qualifying us to share the gospel with others.

DEFINITIONS FOR OUR STUDY

Justification—Justification is the foundational, saving element in the plan of salvation. It is the process whereby God replaces our sinful life record with the righteous merits of Christ's obedient life and atoning death. God does it in accordance with the biblical principle of substitution, which lies at the heart of the sacrificial system (i.e., sacrificial lamb). Ellen White explained justification with these words: "Christ's character stands in place of [as a substitute for] your character, and you are accepted before God just as if you had not sinned" (*Steps to Christ,* p. 62). Justification is based entirely on the work God has done on behalf of the human race in the person of Jesus Christ. We receive justification as we confess our sinful lives to

Christ and by faith accept His salvation as a free gift. Once we receive justification, God considers us to be as perfect as Christ. Human efforts have no justifying merit in us and can do nothing toward establishing justification.

Sanctification—Sanctification is an aspect of the plan of salvation whereby human beings cooperate with the Lord's efforts to save them through justification. We demonstrate our cooperation through our continual faith in Christ's merits to save us. This truth about God's unfailing love for us encourages us so much that we gladly seek to obey the Lord's law, His ten commandments. The changes that take place in our lives through sanctification serve as a witness to others of God's power to save.

However, sanctification contributes no merit toward saving righteousness (that's what justification does). Thus our cooperative works cannot save us. Nevertheless, without our cooperation in the sanctification process Christ cannot possibly justify us before the universe. Our unwillingness to cooperate with God by seeking to bring our lives in harmony with the principles of His law demonstrates the fact that we are still in a state of rebellion against Him. Professed faith without a corresponding respect for God's law is only presumption.

Glorification—Glorification is the process whereby God performs the final act of changing our fallen natures so that we might enter immortal life. It takes place at Christ's second coming when "this corruptible must put on incorruption, and this mortal must put on immortality" (1 Cor. 15:53). Because "flesh and blood [fallen, or carnal, nature] cannot inherit the kingdom of God" (verse 50), the total eradication of our carnal natures will occur at glorification. Then we are in a condition in which we can live with God for eternity. Again it is something that only God can do. It occurs apart from any human effort at the time of Christ's appearing.

CART BEFORE THE HORSE?

We have all heard the saying that "we shouldn't put our cart before our horse." It means that we have all the components necessary to get the job done, but are trying to use them in the wrong order or a way never intended. Obviously, the cart cannot pull the horse, nor can the horse bear all the cargo of the cart. But put the horse in front of the cart and then you can go to market!

This simple illustration depicts the Christian church's agelong struggle to understand the plan of salvation properly. The Lord gave it all the necessary theological components (justification, sanctification, and glorification), but the devil has masterfully kept it from properly applying them. Many have confused the work of justification with that of sanctification, and sanctification with glorification. As long as the church remains confused on these points it will never be able to deliver the gospel cargo to the marketplace of the world.

The servant of the Lord wrote about the devil's strategy to cause confusion on these points: "The danger has been presented to me again and again of entertaining, as a people, false ideas of justification by faith. I have been shown for years that Satan would work in a special manner to confuse the mind on this point [of what justification really is]. . . . I have been shown that many have been kept from the faith because of the mixed, confused ideas of salvation" (*Faith and Works,* p. 18).

In fact, Ellen White went through her own experience of confusion on these points. "My ideas concerning justification and sanctification were confused. These two states were presented to my mind as separate and distinct from each other; yet I failed to comprehend the difference or understand the meaning of the terms, and all the explanations of the preachers increased my difficulties" (*Testimonies for the Church,* vol. 1, p. 23).

The key to victory, in both our personal experience and that of the church at large, will be found in correctly understanding these various theological concepts and how they relate to each other in the salvation process. The devil is determined that we shall never do it. He knows that such knowledge will spiritually set us free. Notice this statement concerning what shall happen when we rightly understand justification's relationship to the plan of salvation. "The enemy of God and man is not willing that this truth [justification] should be clearly presented; for he knows that if the people receive it fully, his power will be broken" (*Gospel Workers,* p. 161).

For years Satan has been fighting within Adventism to deny justification by faith its rightful place. In 1890 we received this clear statement revealing his strategy to confuse justification with what takes place within us through our efforts to keep the law. "The danger has been presented to me again and again of entertaining, as a people, false ideas of justification by faith. I have been shown for years that Satan would work in a special manner to confuse the mind on this point. The law of God has been largely dwelt upon and has been presented to congregations, almost as destitute of the knowledge of Jesus Christ and His relation to the law as was the offering of Cain. I have been shown that many have been kept from the faith because of the mixed, confused ideas of salvation, because ministers have worked in a wrong manner to reach hearts. The point that has been urged upon my mind for years is the imputed righteousness of Christ [justification]. I have wondered that this matter was not made the subject of discourses in our churches throughout the land, when the matter has been kept so constantly urged upon me, and I have made it the subject of nearly every discourse and talk I have given to the people. . . . There is not a point that needs to be dwelt upon more earnestly, repeated more frequently, or established more firmly in the minds of all than the impossibility of fallen man meriting anything by his own best good works. Salvation is through faith in Jesus Christ alone" (*Faith and Works,* pp. 18, 19).

Now let us behold the plan of salvation as God designed it to operate.

THE SURE FOUNDATION—JUSTIFICATION

Before Adam chose to sin, he was in a righteous state of being before God. He could have continued to develop a righteous character by obeying God's law. But after he willfully decided not to trust God, a decision revealed through his disobedience, he placed himself in an unrighteous state (carnal nature). No longer could his obedience to the law secure for him a righteous standing before God. Also, he could pass on to his children only the same fallen nature that he now possessed. Therefore, all his descendants were like him in that by trying to do good they could never return to a holy state of being and eradicate their carnal natures (see *Steps to Christ,* p. 62).

It is the predicament that every one of us finds ourselves in when we enter the world. Our good works can never change the fact that we have a nature that is at "enmity against God" (Rom. 8:7). Like a tree cut off at the stump only to sprout new shoots, no matter how good we try to be, any new growth we might have is still tainted by the sap of our carnal roots. Though we don't realize it, carnal selfishness and pride spoils every good thing that we do. "Christ is the sinner's only hope. There is no comfort for the soul in looking at the good works he has done; for they are all mixed with pride and sin, and by the works of the law shall no flesh be justified in His sight" (*Review and Herald,* June 14, 1892). Isaiah stated that "all our righteousnesses are as filthy rags" (Isa. 64:6). Our efforts at doing good will never avail in saving us. It doesn't get at the root of the problem.

Like that of a helpless young bird fallen from its nest, the human race's only hope lies in someone else's ability to pick them up and place them back in the nest. That someone is Jesus Christ. Although still remaining God, He appeared as a man. However, His humanity did not consist of that carnal element. While our hearts are "at war with the principles of God's law" (*The Great Controversy,* p. 467), Christ could state, "I delight to do thy will, O my God; yea, thy law is within my heart" (Ps. 40:8). Therefore, because He did not possess carnal humanity His obedience to the law of God as a human being formed for Him a righteous character, something we could not do in our carnal state.

Now, because of His eternal love for us, He has made His righteous character, which He wrought out in human nature, available for each of us to use as a substitute. If we by faith accept it as a free gift, then His record of perfect obedience replaces our imperfect record in the books of heaven.

What's more, He suffered the death that we deserve so that we now can possess the eternal life that is rightfully His. Just as the Israelites escaped the judgment that fell upon Egypt by applying the shed blood of a substitute lamb to their doorposts, so "Christ our passover is sacrificed for us" (1 Cor. 5:7). If we give up on our prideful efforts to prove ourselves "good enough," and accept Christ as "the Lord our Righteousness" (Jer. 23:6), then His shed blood will cover us in the day of final judgment. Symbolically speaking, being under Christ's blood means that His perfect character stands in place of our faulty ones, and on that basis we pass the judgment and inherit eternal life.

BEARING FRUIT—SANCTIFICATION

At justification, God plants the seed of His divine nature within us. It germinates, begins to take root, and through the process of sanctification grows up into a fruit-bearing plant. The spiritual fruit matures for the harvest (glorification).

Sanctification, once again, is the result of our believing by faith in the merits of Christ to save (justification). This truth creates within us a desire to cooperate with God through obedience to His will. But we couldn't obey God, nor even have the desire to, without His aid. The Holy Spirit provides the motive. Yet even though the Holy Spirit is involved, the resulting obedience is imperfect because it is mixed with the selfishness and pride associated with our "corrupt channels of humanity" (*Selected Messages,* book 1, p. 344). Our efforts, even prompted by the Holy Spirit, always fall short of meeting the perfect standard that the law of God holds before us.

But we do not despair over this fact, because our hopes for salvation now rest on the sure foundation of justification. It makes up for our feeble efforts at doing what is right. "When it is in the heart to obey God, when efforts are put forth to this end, Jesus accepts this disposition and effort as man's best service, and He makes up for the deficiency with His own divine merit [justification]. But He will not accept those who claim to have faith in Him, and yet are disloyal to His Father's commandment" (*Signs of the Times,* June 16, 1890).

This is the way it will be all the way to the Second Coming—as long as we are still residing in carnal nature. Though victories over many visible sins will progressively take place in our lives, we still are infected with that base nature of carnal pride and selfishness. God will totally remove this nature only through glorification.

When we confuse sanctification with justification, we at some point begin to trust to our obedience as the underlying basis or hope of being made right with God. It's as if we are saying that the time will come when we will bear such perfect, sanctified fruit that we will no longer need the initial justification that undergirded us in the beginning. But this makes no more sense than saying that once my tomato plant begins to bear fruit, it no longer needs its root system. Christ told us that "as the branch cannot bear fruit of itself, except it abide in the vine; no more can ye, except ye abide in me [through justification]. I am the vine, ye are the branches: . . . without me ye can do nothing" (John 15:4, 5).

The key here is abiding in Christ through justification. We do this by forever trusting in His substitute merits as the only reason for our salvation. If the gospel's purpose is only to get me back to a certain level of righteousness, and then abandon me to stand on the foundation of the good work that has taken place within me, then it would be a temporary gospel. But the angel of Revelation has declared it to be an "everlasting gospel" (Rev. 14:6). That means that the foundation of Christ's justifying merits will uphold me throughout eternity.

Nevertheless, my efforts of sanctified obedience are necessary if I really expect the plan of salvation through justification to work for me. When Christ justifies me with His righteousness, it places me in the eyes of God back in the sinless position Adam held before the Fall. I am "made clean" by the fact that He has by His Word declared Jesus' righteousness for my sins that are past (see John 15:3 and Rom. 3:25). Of course I do not realize this in a tangible way, because I am still dwelling in carnal nature. I now see only through that "glass, darkly." When I view Him "face to face" at glorification, it will become a living reality (1 Cor. 13:12). But by faith I can now believe it is so, because God has said it. "There is therefore now no condemnation to them which are in Christ Jesus, who walk not after the flesh, but after the Spirit" (Rom. 8:1).

Often we lose faith in justification because we so often fail in our attempts to overcome sin. Constantly our carnal consciences tell us that we are sinners and unworthy to claim Christianity. But we need not despair. What we need to understand is that "if we confess our sins, he is faithful and just to forgive us our sins, and to cleanse us from all unrighteousness" (1 John 1:9). Notice it says forgiveness takes place as we "confess" our sins, not as we "overcome" them. As a matter of fact, it is impossible ever to hope to overcome a sin unless we first have the assurance that God has already forgiven it.

When Jesus told the woman caught in adultery that she was no longer condemned and that she should "go, and sin no more" (John 8:11), surely He wasn't demanding that she perform as perfectly as Adam did before the Fall. That would have been impossible, because she was still in a carnal state of being. No, what He was telling her was to change her aim. In other words, don't go out planning to sin anymore, but rather intend to do right. "To be led into sin unawares—not intending to sin, but to sin through want of watchfulness and prayer, not discerning the temptation of Satan and so falling into his snare—is very different from the one who plans and deliberately enters into temptation and plans out a course of sin" (*Our High Calling,* p. 177).

Yes, our consciences will always seek to condemn us when we fall short during the sanctification experience. Thank God, we can by faith look beyond our shortcomings and grasp God's justifying forgiveness. "If our heart condemn us, God is greater than our heart, and knoweth all things" (1 John 3:20). However, our "confidence toward God" (1 John 3:21) is destroyed if we purposely pursue a course that we know will defile our conscience (see Titus 1:15, 16). "And herein do I exercise myself, to have always a conscience void of offence toward God, and toward men" (Acts 24:16).

After I am reinstated through Christ to a sinless state before God (remember that we can grasp this only by faith, not by sight), I must make the choice for myself to obey God or not to obey Him. If I choose to obey Him, the Holy Spirit will help me to that end. Once again, even if I fail in my endeavor (which I am often assured to do because of the carnal nature I'm attempting it in), the Lord doesn't hold it against me but covers it with the perfect obedience of Christ through my justification (see 1 John 2:1). The only thing that can ruin the process for me is a willful, determined decision to give up on justification that will in turn lead me to become uncooperative with God. If I do that, then I choose to eat the fruit of the wrong tree (the tree of rebellion), just as Adam did in the beginning. My result will be no different than was his—I will fall from the righteous state I have in Christ.

THE AWAITED HOPE—GLORIFICATION

As a result we should be able to see why "the whole creation groaneth and travaileth in pain together until now. And not only they, . . . even we ourselves groan within ourselves, waiting for the adoption, to wit, the redemption of our body" (Rom. 8:22, 23). The great second advent of our mighty Lord and Savior, Jesus Christ, will release us from the incarceration of our carnal natures. Up to this point the combined work of justification and sanctification have held in check the promptings of the fallen nature. But the warfare that we have faithfully kept up will cease "when he shall come to be glorified in [or to glorify] his saints" (2 Thess. 1:10).

If we die like the thief on the cross before we have a chance to live a lifetime of sanctification, then we will still be glorified at the Second Coming. "These all died in faith [of His justification], not having received the promises [of the eradication of their carnal natures and a home in eternal glorification], but having seen them afar off, and were persuaded of them, embraced them. . . . Wherefore God is not ashamed to be called their God: for he hath prepared for them a city" (Heb. 11:13-16). They will receive those promises at the last trump as God summons them from their graves (1 Thess. 4:14-17).

Those still living at that time shall, like Elijah, receive their glorification without experiencing death (see again verses 14-17). Many refer to them as the 144,000. Much debate has raged about their spiritual state. Some have regarded them as becoming so fully sanctified so as to actually live in a sinless state before the Second Advent. But such a speculative theory disrupts the sensitive balance of the gospel plan that we have been discussing. In order for such a concept to be realistic their carnal natures would have to vanish before the Second Coming. But the Bible states that it is only at His coming that corruptible nature shall put on incorruption. As long as we have a carnal nature, we cannot possibly be in a "sinless" spiritual state, even though we are not willfully yielding to the demands of our rebellious natures.

"While sin is forgiven in this life [through justification], its results [the carnal nature] are not now wholly removed. It is at His coming that Christ is to 'change our vile body [our carnal vessels], that it may be fashioned like unto his glorious body.' Philippians 3:21" (*Selected Messages,* book 2, p. 33). Again, "we cannot say, 'I am sinless,' till this vile body is changed and fashioned like unto His glorious body" (*Signs of the Times,* Mar. 23, 1888).

The heresy that we must become absolutely perfect, matching the perfection of Christ's character, is a soul-destroying device. It will either lead us to give up on the work of sanctification from discouragement, or cause us ultimately to deceive ourselves in believing the lie that we can become perfectly sinless in this lifetime. "There are many, especially among those who profess holiness, who compare themselves to Christ, as though they were equal with Him in perfection of character. This is blasphemy. Could they obtain a view of Christ's righteousness, they would have a sense of their own sinfulness and imperfection" (*Review and Herald,* Mar. 15, 1887). The truth is that the work of "perfecting Christian character after the divine model [through sanctification] . . . will progress in his [the sinner's] character until faith is lost in sight, and grace in glory [at glorification]" (*Signs of the Times,* May 16, 1895).

If I think I must be absolutely perfect in order to be ready for the Second Advent, an honest look at myself will drive me to pray that the Lord will hold it off. But if I understand Christ's coming to be the point at which God releases me from my imperfect carnal nature, then I pray, "Even so, come, Lord Jesus" (Rev. 22:20). Only the latter will fill me with enthusiasm to do what the Lord has asked me to do—to proclaim His second advent to this world.

Surely the old hymn said it right: "O that will be glory for me!"

THE GOSPEL CART GOES TO MARKET—ON A TRAIN!

We have discussed the importance of correctly using the gospel components of justification, sanctification, and glorification in their intended theological functions. Just as only putting the horse in front of the cart can bring us the results we desire, so making sure we have our theological components straightened out is vital if we really want to realize the gospel's full power.

In conclusion, let us consider another analogy that will help sort these issues out. We all know the role that trains have had hauling cargo from one point to another. Yet trains could not function without tracks. In the same way, the gospel train will never travel clear around the world and on to glory until its tracks are properly laid.

Let us consider a set of train tracks. It has two rails running parallel, yet held together by ties. To alter or modify the design would derail the train. The rails must remain in their parallel positions for the system to work. If you try to merge them, or separate them further than their design calls for, you wreck the train. As a matter of fact, that's the major function of the ties. They make sure the rails stay in their intended positions.

It's the same way with justification and sanctification. We can represent them by the two rails. Although they each are "separate and distinct" from each other, they must remain closely tied together to work. If you ever merge the two, the gospel train derails. To separate them further from each other than they should be will also lead to disaster. They must stay tied together, in their appointed place, for the system to function the way God designed it should.

When we have the two rails of justification and sanctification properly laid, then the gospel train can move down the track at amazing speed to its final destination—glorification! And what a wonderful event that will be when God pulls our weary locomotives in through those heavenly gates to the celestial train station of heaven.

What do the railroad ties connecting the two rails of justification and sanctification together represent? They symbolize love. Understanding His great love for us, as expressed through His great gift of justification, elicits our love for God. Love for our fellow human beings also results as we assume God's unjudgmental and merciful attitude and unselfishly bestow it upon others. True love causes us to live unselfishly for the good of others in an attempt to get them aboard the glory-bound train. Here is really the sum and substance of sanctification.

Sometimes it is painful to die to self through sanctification, but it was also painful for Jesus to die for our justification. Maybe that's where the railroad spikes fit in, as infinite wisdom hammers this selfless love into our selfish hearts. "I am crucified with Christ; nevertheless I live; yet not I, but Christ liveth in me: and the life which I now live [sanctified living for others] in the flesh [my carnal state of being] I live by the faith of the Son of God [justification], who loved me, and gave himself for me" (Gal. 2:20).

Sometimes it seems terribly confusing and difficult, but that results from the erroneous and preconceived ideas and opinions that we have all picked up while traveling through the religious landscapes of our past. When we finally understand the roles of each gospel component, we will realize that we have been riding like hobos when we could have gone first-class. We will see that we have been worrying too much about being saved, thus keeping our focus on ourselves. Justification clears this up by giving us an eternal assurance of eternal life. That in turn frees us to live for others in an attempt to share with them the good news we have ourselves received. Thus we get our horse in front of our cart. Then our hearts will thrill with the ability to point other people to the right train as we give the final boarding call to our world.

Salvation is closer than you think. All aboard?

Chapter 6

WAITING ON A FRIEND

One of the things Christians have difficulty understanding is the purpose behind life's trials. Oftentimes such difficulties seem to increase when a person accepts Christ as Savior. Without a clear understanding of the salvation process we cannot really understand why God allows troubles to come our way. As a result, we become impatient as did Israel's king during an incident in the days of Elisha the prophet.

The Syrian king Ben-hadad had besieged Samaria. It triggered a famine so great that people began to eat their own children to survive. Like everyone else, Israel's king waited for God to intervene. But the situation only continued to go from bad to worse. Finally the impatient king lost his confidence in God and, coming to Elisha, exploded, "Look at our plight! This is the Lord's doing. Why should I wait any longer for him to help us?" (2 Kings 6:33, NEB).

Even now, many of us find ourselves going through trials that sometimes seem unbearable. It often appears as though God has forsaken or otherwise forgotten about us. But we need to look behind that dark curtain to discover His purpose in it all.

At times our experience is sunny. But then our sun sets and darkness settles in. Discouragement, fear, and uncertainty replace gladness, peace, and security. During such times of darkness we have the best opportunity to grow in our faith by trusting in God's promises, even though we may see no signs of their fulfillment. Just as we know the sun is sure to rise in the earthly sky and dispel the blackness of night, so we can expect that same cycle in the Christian life. Though it often gets darkest before the dawn, it is only an indicator that light is on its way. Our challenge is to learn to patiently wait upon the Lord "until the day dawn, and the day star [our hope in Christ] arise in your heart" (2 Peter 1:19).

Isaiah went through a similar experience when it appeared to him that God had forsaken his people. "And I will wait upon the Lord, that hideth his face from the house of Jacob, and I will look for him" (Isa. 8:17). Likewise, one of the greatest challenges God's people will face during the shaking will be to maintain patiently their confidence in an unseen God to save them. For the saints during the end of time things are sure to get worse before they get better. The darkness of a wicked world will settle around them. But then Jesus, the light of the world, will return and usher in the eternal morning and take His faithful ones to a world without night (Rev. 21:25).

OUR SOURCE OF STRENGTH

In our last chapter we discussed the necessity to distinguish between justification, sanctification, and glorification. Failing to distinguish carefully between the components of salvation will ultimately lead us into the dark religion of Babylon, a religion of confusion about our spiritual standing with God. Such an experience weakens our faith. But as we sort out these gospel components our faith will grow ever stronger.

Once again the doctrine of justification is the key to obtaining and maintaining positive spiritual growth. That's why it has served as the foundation of every great revival that has taken place among God's people. It has sustained many a martyr during their last earthly testimony for Jesus. Justification takes place only as we realize our spiritual weakness and depravity and trust entirely in the merits of Christ as a complete substitute for us.

Many have viewed the period of sanctification (the time between justification and glorification) as a time to get good enough so as to obtain salvation. *But sanctification is not about trying to gain our salvation but rather about trying to hold on to it.* The sanctification period is when the Lord allows Satan to test our faith in justification. It is Satan's window of opportunity to try to destroy our faith in the justifying merits of Jesus Christ. If he fails, then his temptations will have served only to strengthen our trust in our Savior.

Several Bible texts bring this important truth to light. Hebrews 3:14 declares: "For we are made partakers of Christ, if we hold the beginning of our confidence [of a right standing with God through justification] steadfast unto the end [glorification]." (See also verse 6.)

Paul also taught this vital lesson to the Colossians. He told them that through justification Christ would present them "holy and unblameable and unreproveable in his [God the Father's] sight: if ye continue in the faith [trusting in Christ's justifying merits] grounded and settled, and be not moved away from the hope of the gospel [glorification], which ye have heard" (Col. 1:22, 23).

Christ revealed the same truth to John the revelator. "Behold, I come quickly: hold that fast which thou hast [the promise of being justified in God's eyes through the merits of Christ's blood], that no man take thy crown. He that overcometh will I make a pillar in the temple of my God" (Rev. 3:11, 12).

Here is the real essence of overcoming—to withstand the devil's temptations to give up our faith in justification! He seeks to weaken our faith by two covert methods. Satan tries to convince us that we are too bad to be saved, or that we are too good to be lost. If people believe either lie, they will abandon their total dependence on Christ's justifying power. It is what the Bible calls the sin of unbelief (Heb. 4:11).

In fact, the sin of unbelief is the sin against the Holy Spirit that has no forgiveness. Not because God arbitrarily chooses not to forgive, but because we choose not to believe and accept the only forgiveness made available to us. If we believe we are too bad to be saved, then we doubt Christ's ability "to save them to the uttermost that come unto God by him" (Heb. 7:25). Or if we conclude that we are too good to be lost, then we qualify as Laodiceans. They placed their trust in their own goodness, in their ability to perform certain religious duties, in what is taking place within them, and not in what the Savior did in their behalf on Calvary.

Such experiences can never lead us to have Christ formed within by faith (see Gal. 4:19). Instead they will lead us to a "form of godliness [through outward behavior], but denying the power thereof [the power of Christ to justify us by His life and death]" (2 Tim. 3:5). Scripture counsels us to "turn away" from such an experience.

We need to instead follow Abraham's example. "He staggered not at the promise of God through unbelief; but was strong in faith, giving glory to God; and being fully persuaded that, what he [God] had promised, he was able also to perform. And therefore it was imputed to him for righteousness. Now it was not written for his sake alone, that it [righteousness] was imputed to him; but for us also, to whom it shall be imputed, if we believe on him that raised up Jesus our Lord from the dead; who was delivered for our offences, and was raised again for our justification" (Rom. 4:20-25).

THE PATIENCE OF THE SAINTS

Justification is a transaction that we can know only by faith. "Now faith is the substance of things hoped for, the evidence of things not seen" (Heb. 11:1). The assurance of being made right with God is not something we can see but rather something we by faith believe. The Bible teaches that not only is this the way it will be at the beginning of our walk with Jesus, but it will remain our experience all the way until our faith becomes sight at glorification.

Here is where the "patience of the saints" comes in, as they wait for their glorification (which some will realize through death). Then the Lord will tangibly give them what they have all along believed by faith. That's why it is justification by faith, not justification by sight. The Old Testament prophet Habakkuk declared: "For the vision [experiencing by sight our justification with God] is yet for an appointed time [at glorification], but at the end [when Christ returns] it shall speak, and not lie: though it tarry, wait for it; because it will surely come, it will not tarry. Behold, his soul which is lifted up is not upright in him: but the just shall live by his faith [not by sight]" (Hab. 2:3, 4).

The Christian's greatest challenge is to learn to live by faith and not feeling. Faith is to lead feeling, not the other way around. If we trust to our feelings as to whether or not we are right with God, we will surely shipwreck our faith. We must exercise faith in the merits of Christ regardless of how we feel. At times we may not feel like a Christian. Discouragement, despondency, apathy, rejection, or a hundred other depressing human emotions may threaten to overwhelm us. Other times we get impatient with the speed of God's process. We want our sinless, glorified experience now, and if God won't give it to us, then we will devise a theology to get it ourselves. Thus we choose to believe that through sanctification we can become perfectly sinless in this life, prior to glorification. So we condition our thoughts so as to feel holy because we do things right and others do them wrong. Such feelings deceive us into thinking we have obtained an elite status among God's people. But as Habakkuk said, "his soul which is lifted up is not upright in him," because he is not living by faith (verse 4).

True faith pierces through all such feelings, whether it involves how bad we are (unworthiness) or how good we are (worthiness), and places total trust and hope in the merits (worthiness) of the Son of God. Thus we will never find lasting security in what we perceive is taking place in our life, but rather through accepting by faith what took place in the life of Jesus Christ.

The faith the apostle Paul taught the Galatians to live by is the same faith that will sustain us through storm and trial until our glorification. "I am crucified with Christ: nevertheless I live; yet not I, but Christ liveth in me [through faith]: and the life which I now live in the flesh [in an experience of unreliable human feelings and emotions] I live by the faith [promise of justification] of the Son of God, who loved me, and gave himself for me" (Gal. 2:20). "For we through the Spirit wait for the hope of righteousness by faith" (Gal. 5:5). In other words, we must patiently wait until glorification, the time when the righteousness we now have by faith becomes righteousness by sight.

So the devil will try anything he can to shake our faith in Christ as our justifier. Speaking of the temptations Satan employs to shake our faith, the book of James says: "My brethren, count it all joy when ye fall into divers temptations; knowing this, that the trying of your faith worketh patience" (James 1:2, 3). Such patience is what that king of Israel lacked during the siege of Samaria. How will it be when the devil lays siege upon us and we feel cut off from God? Will our faith in Christ be strong enough to weather the enemy's attacks? Will we have the patience of Job, or will we give up our faith based on what we sense has gone wrong?

Remember that after describing all kinds of terrible repercussions we might face for following Him, Jesus said that "in your patience possess ye your souls" (Luke 21:19). Come what may, it is imperative that we maintain our faith in Christ's power to save us through His merits alone until our hopes are realized in glorification. Said the apostle: "And we desire that every one of you do shew the same diligence to the full assurance of hope [of justification giving way to glorification] unto the end [till Christ's appearing]: that ye be not slothful, but followers of them who through faith and patience inherit the promises. For . . . God made promise to Abraham. . . . And so, after he [Abraham] had patiently endured, he obtained the promise" (Heb. 6:11-15).

Once again, as we review the patriarch's life record, we do not see a perfect performance but a faith that was in the process of being perfected. So it will be with us. Many times during our lifelong sanctification process we will fall short of our own expectations, yet we need not despair. The prophet Isaiah foretold that such disheartening experiences will serve only to strengthen our faith as we return to the source of hope, the merits of our Savior, Jesus. Speaking of such experiences, he said: "He giveth power to the faint; and to them that have no might he increaseth strength. Even the youths shall faint and be weary, and the young men shall utterly fall: but they that wait upon the Lord shall renew their strength [their assurance of acceptance through Christ]; they shall mount up with wings as eagles; they shall run, and not be weary; and they shall walk, and not faint" (Isa. 40:29-31).

WHAT ARE YOU WAITING FOR?

Before the end comes, it will appear as though the wicked will prosper and the righteous will perish. But according to Scripture, this too is only a test. The psalmist declared: "Fret not thyself because of evildoers, neither be thou envious against the workers of iniquity. For they shall soon be cut down like the grass, and wither as the green herb. Trust in the Lord [justification], and do good [sanctification]. . . . Commit thy way unto the Lord [sanctification]; trust also in him [justification]; and he shall bring it to pass [glorification]. And he shall bring forth thy righteousness as the light, and thy judgment as the noonday. Rest in the Lord [or take spiritual rest in His merits], and wait patiently for him. . . . Fret not thyself in any wise to do evil [in other words, live your life by sanctified principles and not by the examples of the unrighteous]. For evildoers shall be cut off: but those that wait upon the Lord [until glorification], they shall inherit the earth" (Ps. 37:1-9).

So we see that it is a waiting game. That's what Jesus meant when He said: "And ye shall be hated of all men for my name's sake: but he that endureth to the end shall be saved" (Matt. 10:22). Thank God, we need not wait in uncertainty, but we can have the assurance of our salvation all the while through justification. Justification imparts to us the desire to live a sanctified life until the time of Jesus' appearing and glorification takes place.

In fact, Paul said that the whole creation is waiting for the time of glorification. It is this hope that encourages us to willfully and joyfully endure sufferings in the present life. "We are God's heirs and Christ's fellow-heirs, if we share in his sufferings now in order to share his splendour hereafter. For I reckon that the sufferings we now endure bear no comparison with the splendour, as yet unrevealed, which is in store for us. For the created universe waits with eager expectation for God's sons to be revealed [at glorification]. . . . Up to the present, we know, the whole created universe groans in all its parts as if in pangs of childbirth. Not only so, but even we, to whom the Spirit is given as firstfruits of the harvest to come, are groaning inwardly while we wait for God to make us his sons and set our whole body free. For we have been saved, though only in hope [or by faith in justification]. Now to see is no longer to hope: why should a man endure and wait for what he already sees? But if we hope for something we do not yet see, then, in waiting for it, we show our endurance" (Rom. 8:17-25, NEB).

Notice here the part that the Holy Spirit plays. It is His job to lead us to trust in Christ through good times and bad, all the while encouraging us that it will all end on a right note called glorification. That is why Scripture calls Him the Comforter. When we reach the place in our fight against evil that we feel we cannot hang on any longer, the Spirit comes to our rescue. He renews our strength by renewing our hope. "Now the God of hope fill you with all joy and peace in believing [in justification], that you may abound in hope, through the power of the Holy Ghost" (Rom. 15:13). The Spirit's sustaining of our hope in justification is how Christ fulfills His promise to be with us "alway, even unto the end of the world" (Matt. 28:20).

"And it shall be said in that day, Lo, this is our God; we have waited for him, and he will save us: this is the Lord; we have waited for him, we will be glad and rejoice in his salvation" (Isa. 25:9).

Chapter 7

THE STRAIGHT TESTIMONY AND THE SEALING

It was a bright and glorious Sabbath morning as my wife and I awoke in a Tennessee motel room. We were traveling through the state and had stopped over for the Sabbath. After locating the local Adventist church, we made it in time for Sabbath school. But we were totally unprepared for what would happen.

The lesson study was on the subject of how to be a good witness for Christ. Midway through the study a young woman named Karen brought up the subject of dress. After reading several select statements from Ellen White, she turned to the other women in the church and rebuked them for wearing slacks and pants. Of course, this only provoked them into condemning her for her extremism. Within moments the entire room broke out in angry controversy. In the midst of it all, a man sitting next to me stood and shouted, "It's the shaking, Karen. Give the straight testimony and stand your ground, even though the dragon roars!"

Needless to say, I'll never forget that morning. But the question has since often come to my mind: Was Karen really giving what we call, in Adventist jargon, the straight testimony? Does the straight testimony center on what we eat or wear? Or does the phrase have a deeper, more significant, spiritual meaning?

THE TRUE WITNESS

The phrase "straight testimony" actually comes from page 270 of the book *Early Writings* in a chapter entitled "The Shaking." In this chapter Ellen White said she saw in vision God's people engaged in an intense warfare against Satan and his evil angels. At times darkness would totally surround them. But a ray of light from Jesus would break through, giving them hope and courage to continue in their struggle. She claimed that she saw "angels of God hasten to the assistance of all who were struggling with all their power to resist the evil angels and trying to help themselves by calling upon God with perseverance. But His angels left those who made no effort to help themselves, and I lost sight of them." Then she wrote the part about the straight testimony. "I asked the meaning of the shaking I had seen and was shown that it would be caused by the straight testimony called forth by the counsel of the True Witness to the Laodiceans. This [the testimony] will have its effect upon the heart of the receiver, and will lead him to exalt the standard and pour forth the straight truth. Some will not bear this straight testimony. They will rise up against it, and this is what will cause a shaking among God's people" (*Early Writings,* p. 270).

Although I have read this chapter for many years and never really understood its real meaning, I now believe I know what God was trying to get across through the vision. Notice who sends the straight testimony and whom it is being sent to. From the True Witness (Jesus) it goes to the Laodiceans. Ellen White would later in her ministry make clear that this message to the Laodiceans was justification by faith. "The Laodicean message has been sounding. Take this message in all its phases and sound it forth to the people wherever Providence opens the way. Justification by faith and the righteousness of Christ are the themes to be presented to a perishing world" (*The Ellen G. White 1888 Materials,* vol. 3, p. 1054).

Of course, the scriptural allusion directs our attention to the third chapter of the book of Revelation. There Jesus gives a message of love and warning to a people who think they are spiritually healthy and wealthy but in reality are sick and destitute. And it's all because they have left Jesus standing outside the door to their religious experience. Jesus is the true witness, and we are the Laodiceans. The reason we are Laodiceans is that we have received the message of salvation through Christ only as an intellectual fact. Unable to understand its fullness through experience, we view our forgiveness and release from condemnation only as a necessary stepping-stone on our journey to mortal perfection—and not as an all-encompassing truth. Thus we conclude that our real hope lies in what can eventually be accomplished in us and not in what has been done for us in the person of Christ.

Many of us were told we need not be perfect to join the Adventist Church. But soon after our baptism, some began to claim that we had to get perfect before the close of probation if we wanted to remain with those going to heaven. For those of us who naturally possessed strong willpower the task of overcoming our outward defects was no problem. We seemed to sail over every obstacle that confronted us. As a matter of fact, we just couldn't understand why others struggled so hard to overcome their lifelong habits. After all, it was only a simple matter of praying to God for help and then getting up and doing it.

But we were unwittingly being deceived into what the apostle Paul termed "will worship" (Col. 2:23). That is, we mistake the power of our own wills for that of the Holy Spirit. But the Holy Spirit's job is not to show us how spiritually strong we are, but how spiritually weak. He never tries to convince us that we can become perfect in this lifetime. Rather, His most difficult task is somehow to convince those of us who have fallen into the trap of worshiping the power of our own wills that we cannot become inherently perfect before Christ returns. Then—and only then—will we see our continual need of the gospel.

To accomplish this, the Spirit leads us to read the "testimony of Jesus" as penned by the various prophets. Something in these testimonies reaches in and identifies with our experience. Step by step we come to acknowledge the eternal verity that salvation is by grace through faith in Jesus Christ alone, from start to finish. We realize that Jesus is not only the author of our faith, but also its finisher. In other words, the means of our salvation is the same at the end of our journey as it was at the beginning. It is all by imputed grace. Now we begin to recognize that all the overcoming we did—though indeed beneficial to us in living a more productive life—also fed our religious pride. At the same time we grasp the vital fact that all we have overcome is nothing compared to the overcoming of our pitiful self-righteousness by relying solely on the merits of Christ for our eternal security. Though still convinced of the commonsense logic behind the counsels stemming from God's holy law, the gospel of grace becomes our constant meat and drink. We then engage our whole energies in trying to help other people to see it.

This is what Ellen White was referring to when she said the testimony will "have its effect upon the heart of the receiver, and will lead him to exalt the standard [the perfect, matchless life of Christ] and pour forth the straight truth" (*Early Writings,* p. 270). But she also said some will not bear this straight testimony (that our works don't count for salvation) and will resist it. Surely that could never happen in Adventism—or could it?

THE TESTIMONY IN HISTORY

If we objectively search the history of the Seventh-day Adventist Church, we will find a people too focused on their own observance of the law. We also discover a God who has been trying to get Adventists to focus on Jesus and His accomplishments in their behalf. In fact, from the period of 1844 to 1888 the church was steeped in outright legalism. That's why Ellen White, in that same chapter of *Early Writings,* wrote: "I saw that the testimony of the True Witness has not been half heeded. The solemn testimony [of justification by faith] upon which the destiny of the church hangs has been lightly esteemed, if not entirely disregarded. This testimony must work deep repentance; all who truly receive it will obey it and be purified" *(ibid.).*

That testimony of Christ came to the church in a dramatic way during the Minneapolis General Conference session of 1888. But as prophesied, many opposed and rejected it. They also ridiculed as heretics those who preached the message. Such Adventists had become conditioned to think that the most important thing for salvation was human obedience to the law. They regarded any message that sought to place the emphasis on the grace of Christ as an attempt to do away with the claims of God's law.

As with Karen and her friend that day at Sabbath school, Adventist leaders in 1888 thought "the straight testimony" would be a stern message of rebuke and reproof of how people were not doing what God expected of them. What they got instead was a message that focused on the love, grace, and mercy of God through what Christ had already done for them. At the same time it indirectly rebuked the spiritual pride they had been cultivating through their lawkeeping. Bypassing all the external facades, it laid the ax at the root of the human tree, the pride of the carnal, or fallen, heart. Those who didn't want to see it tried to refute the message, concluding that it was those who were not keeping the law well enough that needed reproving. Since they obeyed the law, they were all right. Consequently, they began to fight the message of grace under the assumption that they were only preserving the law's paramount position within Adventism.

Speaking of this struggle between the law and the message of justification by faith, Ellen White told the participants at a Bible school in 1890: "When you go from this place, oh be so full of the message [justification by faith] that it is like fire shut up in your bones, that you cannot hold your peace. It is true men will say, 'You are too excited; you are making too much of this matter, and you do not think enough of the law; now, you must think more of the law; don't be all the time reaching for this righteousness of Christ, but build up the law.'" Then she added: "Let the law take care of itself. We have been at work on the law until we get as dry as the hills of Gilboa, without dew or rain. Let us trust in the merits of Jesus Christ of Nazareth. May God help us that our eyes may be anointed with eyesalve, that we may see. . . . Do we believe? Will we come in God's appointed way? May the Lord help us and enlighten us, that we may go forth from this place as they went forth to proclaim the truth after the day of Pentecost; and there were souls converted; they could not resist the testimony" (*The Ellen G. White 1888 Materials,* vol. 2, pp. 557, 558).

THE LAW AND THE GOSPEL COMBINED
But there is indeed a danger of doing away with the claims of

God's law. It was the mistake made by the majority of churches that emerged from the Protestant Reformation. The teaching that "the law has been done away with" was highly popular during the eighteenth, nineteenth, and twentieth centuries.

Jesus said He came not to destroy the law but to fulfill it (Matt. 5:17). It was to establish the principles of His divine law that Christ had to die. If the law had been a disposable or alterable element in God's government, then heaven needed only to lower its standard so as to allow us to enter its eternal courts. But we should always meet such erroneous suggestions with a gracious rebuke, whether they be in the church or in our own minds.

We should never interpret the message of Christ's love, mercy, and grace to mean that He doesn't care about our obedience to His law. Notice this rare but significant statement Ellen White made to a group of conference presidents in an attempt to help them find balance on the law and the gospel: "We must look more to the presentation of God's love and mercy to move the hearts of the people. We must have a sense of both the justice and mercy of God. Those who can blend together the law of God and the mercy of God can reach any heart. For years I have seen that there is a broken link which has kept us from reaching hearts; this link is supplied by presenting the love and mercy of God. There has been a sentiment creeping in that we should not present the claims of the Sabbath so strong. Why not? Is it not true that the man of sin is raising up the counterfeit and undermining the law of God, and should we not raise up the standard against him?" (Ellen G. White to the Council of Presidents meeting, Mar. 3, 1891).

Though we should ever be on guard against antinomianism, those of us who are law-oriented should also be careful not to think that just because someone is preaching grace they are subtly trying to undermine God's law. In fact, it would be a good thing if all law-oriented Adventists checked themselves to make sure their own views are balanced. "There should be deep searching of the Scriptures that the ministers of God may declare the whole counsel of God. The relation of Christ to the law is but faintly comprehended. Some preach the law, and feel that their brethren are not doing their whole duty if they do not present the subject [the law] in the very same way in which they do. These brethren shrink from the presentation of justification by faith, but just as soon as Christ is discovered in His true position to the law, the misconception that has existed on this important matter [justification by faith] will be removed. The law and the gospel are so blended that the truth cannot be presented as it is in Jesus, without blending these subjects in perfect agreement. The law is the gospel of Christ veiled; the gospel of Jesus is nothing more or less than the law defined, showing its far-reaching principles" (*The Ellen G. White 1888 Materials,* vol. 2, p. 674).

Please note here that the key to blending the law and the gospel is the discovery of Christ's "true position to the law." Legalists see the standard of the law as something they can reach through their own Spirit-inspired obedience. They place much emphasis on carrying out the law's demands because it is central to their hope for eternal life. But by holding up our obedience as the standard, we are actually lowering the law's demands. What we need to behold is the relationship of Christ's obedience to the law. That's what the gospel accomplishes. It shows us that our obedience always falls far short of meeting the standard of the law. Then it reveals "the far-reaching principles" of the law by uplifting Christ's infinite level of obedience as the highest standard of lawkeeping.

Though we can imitate Christ's life of obedience, we can never perfectly duplicate it. To think that we can means that we do not yet understand the gospel of grace. Salvation is based on the condition of "perfect obedience to the law of God, perfect righteousness" (*Steps to Christ,* p. 62). If we could at any time match Christ's record, then salvation could rest on our obedience. But "we cannot perfectly obey the holy law" *(ibid.).* In other words, it's not possible for a finite being to satisfy the claims of an infinite law through obedience. That's why "it is by his grace you are saved, through trusting him; it is not your own doing. It is God's gift, not a reward for work done. There is nothing for anyone to boast of. For we are God's handiwork, created in Christ Jesus to devote ourselves to the good deeds for which God has designed us" (Eph. 2:8-10, NEB).

THE SEALING

The seventh chapter of Revelation begins by portraying angelic forces at work in the last days. They are about ready to unleash Satan so that he can make his final attack against our planet. But God has stationed powerful angels "on the four corners of the earth" (Rev. 7:1) to hold the devastation at bay. Then God sends "another angel ascending from the east, having the seal of the living God" (verse 2). That angel instructs the other angels to "hurt not the earth, neither the sea, nor the trees, till we have sealed the servants of our God in their foreheads" (verse 3).

Here we have the seal of the living God. The result of understanding and experiencing this proper balance between the law and the gospel, it affects both the inner and outer person. The seal calls special attention to the great doctrines of justification by faith and the seventh-day Sabbath.

Adventists have often limited their understanding of the seal of God as being the Sabbath. But the Sabbath seal not only represents the law portion of the message that we are to give to the world. The seal of God also involves the message of being justified by His grace through faith. We receive this seal at conversion. It is an experience we continue to grow into until the promised day of our redemption at Christ's coming. We see this in what Paul wrote to the Ephesians concerning the work of the Holy Spirit in bringing an understanding of Christ's forgiveness to them: "And grieve not the Holy Spirit of God, whereby ye are sealed unto the day of redemption. . . . And be ye kind, one to another, tenderhearted, forgiving one another, even as God for Christ's sake hath forgiven you" (Eph. 4:30-32).

Simply put, it works like this. The gospel of redemption through Christ's grace sets a seal upon us as it frees us from the guilt of our sinfulness. Before our conversion we viewed the law as our enemy because it condemned us. But being released from the guilt and condemnation of the law through grace, we come to view the law as a benefactor. We now recognize that it teaches us how to live a life of peace and love. As did David, we can now proclaim: "O how I love thy law! it is my meditation all the day" (Ps. 119:97). Even when we fall short of obeying that law, we do not turn bitter toward its demands. Though we have failed to meet its stipulations, we know it does not condemn us, in light of Christ's covering grace. Through years of experiencing this relationship between the law and grace our love and appreciation for both deepens. The final result is that we arrive at the place in our Christian walk where we depend entirely on justification by grace for our spiritual standing with God, apart from our efforts to obey His law. Yet we also develop such reverence for His will, as expressed through the law, that we would rather die than knowingly violate one of its precepts.

This is the sealing process. Although we receive the seal at conversion, its imprint deepens in our lives as we grow in grace. Through grace we can become so totally committed to God that nothing can sever that relationship. It is what Ellen White was talking about when in reference to the sealing she wrote that the sealing is "a settling into the truth, both intellectually and spiritually, so they cannot be moved" (*The Seventh-day Adventist Bible Commentary,* Ellen G. White Comments, vol. 4, p. 1161). When God's people become thus settled, the final shaking will begin.

Historically, Adventists have believed and taught that the last great test of our faith will be over the Sabbath issue. I totally agree. However, the issue is much deeper than which day we observe as Sabbath. The Sabbath is only like a buoy on a lake. Boats avoid the visible buoy because it alerts them to the fact that something bigger and more serious lurks beneath the water's surface. Likewise, the controversy over God's law (the Sabbath-Sunday issue) only alerts us to the fact of a deeper conflict about how He saves the human race.

Pagan teaching has it that human beings redeem themselves through their own works. Apostolic Christianity taught that humanity is saved by grace through faith alone. The little-horn power of Daniel's vision blended these ideas on salvation and declared that God uses a combination of faith and works. Since a government's authority derives from its law, the Roman church then sought to prove it had the right to change the early church's teachings on salvation by altering God's law. H. F. Thomas, who served as chancellor to Cardinal James Gibbons in 1895, declared: "Of course the Catholic Church claims that the change [the transferral of sacredness from Saturday to Sunday] was her act . . . and the act is a mark of her ecclesiastical power and authority in religious matters." (For further study on the relationship between justification by faith and the Sabbath, see my book *Saving Blood* [Pacific Press Publishing Association, 2000].)

To meet this challenge God has kept His prophetic promise. He explained to Daniel that at the end of the 2300 prophetic days He would begin a movement that would counteract the teachings of this little-horn power (see Dan. 8:14). It would produce a people who understood the proper relationship between law and gospel by uplifting to the world the pristine gospel of salvation by grace alone, accompanied with a call to obedience to all of God's commandments.

It was to this end that God brought the Seventh-day Adventist Church into being. "To the law and to the testimony" will prove to be the battle cry for its success. But before we can give this loud-cry message to the world, we must first become settled and sealed in it ourselves. God has promised a special gift to help us to this end. In our next chapter we shall discover what that special gift is.

Chapter 8

THE LATTER RAIN
AND THE TIME OF TROUBLE

The Bible compares growth in the Christian experience to biological development. We all came into this natural world by passing through water at birth. Likewise, we are "born again" spiritually as we pass through the water of God's grace. As we comprehend the love and mercy God has toward us—His willingness to forgive and forget all our wrongs—a new spiritual life is born within us. By faith we become a new creature in Christ Jesus. But just as a baby is completely helpless and requires total care from others, so we must depend on Christ to nurture us spiritually. We cannot generate even a single spiritual thought unless Christ feeds it to our minds through the Holy Spirit.

As we grow we learn to do right and shun the wrong through the painful process of reaping the harvest of our decisions. "For whatsoever a man soweth, that shall he also reap" (Gal. 6:7). In mercy God allows us to experience both the joy of doing right and the chastisement of doing wrong. But right behavior is not always a sign of spiritual maturity. Sometimes what seems right on the surface actually stems from selfish motivations. Like a good father, therefore, God seeks to purify our motives. Through the process of time He leads us to do right things out of pure motives—love for Him and our fellow human beings.

As we discussed in our previous chapter, Scripture calls this process of spiritual growth the sealing. Leading us to stand for right principles, for the right reasons, is how God intends to keep us from being shaken out when trouble comes our way. It is important we understand this root/fruit relationship between our faith and actions. If we don't, then we will never balance the law and the gospel in our experience. We will be more vulnerable to the devil's attempts to overthrow our faith.

THE ROOT AND ITS FRUIT

The Bible also illustrates our spiritual growth by what happens in the plant kingdom. It speaks of human beings as wheat and tares and compares the planting of spiritual truths in the heart to the sowing of seed. Jesus stated that our spiritual growth was a gradual process, just as the grain plant first develops a stalk, then the head, and finally mature seed (Mark 4:28).

The apostle Paul also employed agrarian metaphors as he sought to teach his converts truths about Christian growth. He talked to the Ephesians about being "rooted and grounded in love" (Eph. 3:17). This concept of the root is key to understanding all other truths about what it means to be a Christian. Jesus is the root that brings life-giving energy to us. Isaiah said He would be to us "as a root out of a dry ground" (Isa. 53:2). In other words, just as the root is the support system for the plant, so reliance on the merits of Jesus' righteousness nourishes our spiritual life.

Deep roots not only provide the tree with the food elements necessary for survival; they also give it stability during storms. When heavy winds blow, trees with shallow root systems are the ones most likely to get uprooted. Similarly, our roots of faith must grow deep into the religion of Christ in order to stand during the shaking. This happens as we experience more fully the truth of justification by faith.

Proverbs 12:3 says: "The root of the righteous shall not be moved." The foliage of our visible commitment may often wither; our fruit may at times appear to be dying on the vine; we may even find ourselves bent to the ground by the trials of life that blow our way; but the Bible says nothing will uproot us. If through justification we remain tapped into that eternal life-giving root, Jesus Christ, then we can outweather anything that comes our way—even death! As Martin Luther wrote in his hymn "A Mighty Fortress": "The body they may kill; God's truth [justification in Christ] abideth still." Yes, though we may go dormant in death, if we have died in the faith our root is still alive. We will resurrect in the spring of the eternal morning.

A plant with a solid root system will naturally bear the fruit its planter intends. Likewise, the Christian rooted in the justifying merits of Jesus Christ will eventually bear the fruit that God intends. Proverbs 12:12 says that "the root of the righteous yieldeth fruit." Jesus said: "Either make the tree good, and his fruit good; or else make the tree corrupt, and his fruit corrupt: for the tree is known by his fruit" (Matt. 12:33). He is of course speaking of the fruits of the Spirit that appear in a person's life as they become more and more acquainted with the salvation of Christ (see Gal. 5:22, 23).

The apostle James said that the life of a Christian would be "full of mercy and good fruits" (James 3:17). Perhaps the greatest evidence that Christian fruit is maturing appears in the way we deal with others. By nature we tend to be hard on each other, showing little mercy. But as we experience more of the root sap of Christ's merciful and forgiving attitude toward our own sinfulness, we become more merciful in our dealings with those who do wrong against us. It is the only way we will ever be able to carry out our commission to love our enemies (Matt. 5:43-48). If we lose sight of what Christ has done for us, we will automatically revert back to our selfish attitudes and actions toward others. Our only hope of becoming and remaining true Christians is a daily living experience in the forgiveness Christ provides for us.

Some never partake of Christ's spirit, because they never accept the forgiveness the Lord has for them. Others seek a religious experience only in an attempt to boost their self-worth. Quickly glossing over their sinfulness and treating the issue of justification as only a prerequisite for joining the church, they are eager to show everyone what they can accomplish in the name of Christ. Becoming too fixated and enamored with their spiritual performance, they set themselves and others up for deception. They are like the showy fig tree that Christ cursed. Though their lives apparently are full of religious fruit, it is the same fruit of self-centeredness that caused humanity's fall in the Garden of Eden.

Fruit is always more attractive than the root that grows it. Its visible beauty and irresistible features attract our attention. That's why produce shops love to display their fruit. It's the same in the spiritual life. Christians are more prone to exalt works than faith in the merits of Christ alone. Most consumers are more drawn to a bushel of apples than the rootstock that can grow them. Likewise, people comment on and exalt the works of others while they count "the blood of the covenant [the root of justification] . . . an unholy thing" (Heb. 10:29).

An incident in a church in which I served as elder brought this fact vividly to my mind a few years ago. After I had preached several sermons on the topic of justification by faith, one of the members reproved me. He thought I gave too much emphasis to the topic and stated that he was sick and tired of hearing everybody in the Adventist Church talking about justification and righteousness by faith. I thought to myself about the Israelites who complained that all they were being fed was manna. They were sick and tired of it. Of course, that manna was an Old Testament type of Christ's life-sustaining energies through His spiritual merits. How could we ever tire of hearing what our Lord has done for us through justification, which, spiritually speaking, is our life support line? I suppose one could go to the other extreme by failing to comment on the spiritual fruit borne out of such a relationship. But I caution us all, as I did that man that day, never to take for granted the importance of the rootstock. Without it, we are Christians in name only. Any fruit that we bear will in the eyes of God be corrupted with selfishness and pride.

LET IT RAIN

God provides natural plants everything necessary to bear their harvest of fruit. He also gives us all the spiritual elements needed to bring forth the fruitful results of a relationship with Him. One of the most essential substances, both in the natural and spiritual realms, is rain.

Because Palestine does not have any permanent rivers for irrigation (except for the Jordan), farmers had to depend totally on rainfall. The success of their crops depended upon it. That's why they prayed so earnestly for it to fall. Palestine has both a dry and a rainy season. The rainy season has two peaks, what the Bible calls the early rain and the latter rain. The storms of early rain come in the late fall and soften the hard soil for plowing and planting. Germinating the seed and bringing it to life, the autumn rains establish the root system and begin the growth process. But the plant could not produce harvestable fruit through the aid of the early rain alone. During the ensuing months the crops will need more life-sustaining moisture. In the spring the cluster of showers termed the latter rain provide that moisture and complete the plant's growth process, bringing it to full fruition. (Note: In the growing season of many other parts of the world the early rains may fall in the spring and the latter showers in late summer or early fall.)

By nature we are dead spiritually. But within all of us God has planted the seed of faith in the heart (Rom. 12:3). That seed lies dormant until we receive the early rain of God's Spirit, at which time spiritual life germinates. This happens as we find forgiveness and peace through the message of Christ's righteousness. We then begin to develop roots of trust and reliance on the fact that God no longer sees us as sinners but as perfectly just. But sooner or later, through the influence of this corrupt world or by the adoption of a more legalistic theology, we hit the drought of summer. We lose our first love as we forget our total dependency on the justifying merits of Christ and become parched through guilt-producing behavior or by our own efforts to become good enough for God. If left unattended by the Spirit of grace, we could no more finish our growth process than could the barley in Boaz's field have matured without the latter rain. God designed this to demonstrate our absolute need for His salvation by grace through faith alone.

The book of Jude offers us a strong word of caution. It warns us about "certain men" who will creep into our fellowship "unawares." Outwardly they will appear to be sincere Christians, but through their teachings they will be "denying the only Lord God, and our Lord Jesus Christ" (Jude 4). Such individuals, though outwardly religious, are anti-gospel. Though they will sit with us at our fellowship meals and speak "great swelling words" (verse 16), Jude compares them to "clouds . . . without water, carried about of winds; trees whose fruit withereth, without fruit, twice dead, plucked up by the roots" (verse 12). In other words, their faith is not rooted in what Christ has done for them, but in what they see themselves as doing for Christ. As a matter of fact, they are so impressed with what they accomplish by themselves that during the executive phase of the judgment Christ will have need to "convince all that are ungodly among them of all their ungodly deeds" (verse 15). No doubt this is the same class that Jesus said would think they were righteous through their deeds and are surprised when He says to them, "I never knew you" (Matt. 7:23).

Jude goes on to instruct us how to combat their deceptive, ungodly influence. "But ye, beloved, building up yourselves on your most holy faith, praying in the Holy Ghost, keep yourselves in the love of God, looking for the mercy of our Lord Jesus Christ unto eternal life" (Jude 20, 21). It was his way of saying, "Stay focused on the forgiveness [justification] Christ has for you."

But like the man who censored me for preaching too much on mercy and grace, many grow weary of hearing this message. They lose sight of its importance. Growing up on a farm, I can tell you that when it rains all the time the farmer no longer appreciates its value. But let a long hard drought come, and the farmer not only begins to pray for rain, but does a dance of jubilation when it finally descends. The Lord sometimes allows the spiritual water supply (message of grace) to be cut off so we will have a correct estimate of its value.

As a Christian, I can testify that I began my journey having no other hope for salvation than the fact that Jesus covered my sinfulness with His righteousness. But after only a few years in the Adventist Church I began to adopt sentiments that shifted my hope to my performance in the Christian life. That's when the drought started. Thankfully, my root system of knowing that salvation was ultimately through Jesus did not die out during those 10 years when no rain fell my way. It kept me from giving up faith altogether during those times when I felt my performance was lacking. What a glorious day it was when the message that Jesus' righteous substitution was all I needed to be assured of my salvation came full circle in my understanding. It was then I rediscovered that by trusting implicitly in the blood of His cross I was at the pinnacle of my Christian experience.

Though it wounded my spiritual pride to admit it, everything I had done as a Christian that I thought was so important and valuable carried no weight when it came to establishing my salvation. The words of Hosea now took on special meaning to me: "Come, and let us return unto the Lord: for he hath torn, and he will heal us; he hath smitten, and he will bind us up. After two days will he revive us: in the third day he will raise us up, and we shall live in his sight. Then shall we know, if we follow on to know the Lord: his going forth is prepared as the morning; and he shall come unto us as the rain, as the latter and former rain unto the earth" (Hosea 6:1-3). It was when the Holy Spirit reinforced the message of Christ's righteousness in my mind that I discovered my "goodness is as a morning cloud, and as the early dew it goeth away" (verse 4). My human attempts at irrigating my religious experience through my own righteous works had brought me no peace. In no way could that experience prepare me for the troublous times that still lie ahead. Only the message of Christ's justifying merits could accomplish that.

THE REFRESHING

In our last chapter we began examining a vision Ellen White recorded in her book *Early Writings,* pages 269-273. We saw there how in the last days evil angels besieged a large group of God's people in an attempt to shut Jesus out of their spiritual view. But some of them had an experience in justification and poured forth "the straight testimony" concerning Christ's essential role in the plan of salvation. Many resisted what they had to say and abandoned the body of believers. Those who did not respect the value of the gift "were left behind in darkness, and their places were immediately filled by others taking hold of the truth and coming into the ranks" (p. 271).

Next we have this commentary on the plight of God's saints at the end of time: "Evil angels still pressed around them, but could have no power over them" *(ibid.)*. Another statement Ellen White would make later on in her ministry sheds light on this vision. She said that Satan knows if believers fully receive the message of justification by faith, "his power [over God's people] will be broken" (*Gospel Workers,* p. 161).

In her *Early Writings* vision she next relates that she "heard those clothed with armor speak forth the truth with great power. . . . All fear of their relatives was gone, and the truth alone was exalted to them. . . . I asked what had made this great change. An angel answered, 'It is the latter rain, the refreshing from the presence of the Lord, the loud cry of the third angel'" (*Early Writings,* p. 271). The vision ends as the empowered group weathers the time of trouble by trusting in the message of salvation through Christ until God saves them from their oppressors at the Second Advent.

Over the years Adventists have frequently discussed the subject of the latter rain. Many have claimed that we must become perfect before we can receive the outpouring of the Holy Spirit in the latter rain and thus be enabled to give the loud cry message. The "holy flesh" and "receive ye the Holy Ghost" movements that appeared around the beginning of the twentieth century were some of the more notable ones. In more recent times the Brinsmead and Shepherd's Rod factions also emphasized perfection. But their followers never reached their goal.

My study of the subject has convinced me that the latter rain is the simple message of justification brought home to the soul by experience. The number one job of the Holy Spirit is to get us to trust entirely on the second member of the Godhead for salvation. The loud cry message is not about being perfect but of dealing realistically with our imperfections by trusting in Christ's merits to cover them.

The fact that we Adventists have had difficulty accepting this truth can once again be best observed in the history of our church at the time of the 1888 Minneapolis session. Before that meeting Adventists were well versed in Ellen White's statements on the law's relationship to perfection. Then during the 1880s Ellet Waggoner introduced the Reformation theological concept of justification to put both the law and grace in their proper places. His writings undermined the law-oriented emphasis of most Adventists. As a result, people fought his books and articles and tried to use certain Ellen White statements from the past to refute it. But much to their surprise, Ellen White sided with the message Waggoner had brought to the session by saying that it was the beginning of the loud cry and outpouring of the latter rain. She stated that regardless of what we had believed and taught in the past, justification by faith was the message for the hour and would continue until the church had proclaimed it to the world.

"The brazen serpent was uplifted in the wilderness that those who looked in faith might be made whole," Ellen White commented. "In like manner God sends a restoring, healing message to men, calling upon them to look away from man and earthly things, and place their trust in God. He has given His people the truth with power through the Holy Spirit. He has opened His Word to those who were searching and praying for truth. But when these messengers gave the truth they had received to the people, they [the Adventist Church members] were as unbelieving as the Israelites. Many are caviling over the truth brought to them by humble messengers. They question, How can this message be truth? How is it possible that by looking to Jesus and believing in His imputed righteousness [justification], I may gain eternal life? Those who have thus refused to see the truth do not realize that it is God with whom they are in controversy, that in refusing the message sent them, they are refusing Christ" (*The Ellen G. White 1888 Materials,* vol. 4, p. 1688).

Undoubtedly, God had all this history recorded so that we will not make the same mistake. It is essential that we realize that the outpouring of the latter rain is what we so desperately need to enable us to fulfill the gospel commission and prepare us for the time of trouble. The apostle Peter clearly indicated that we needed Jesus Christ: "Repent ye therefore, and be converted, that your sins may be blotted out [forgiven], when the times of the refreshing shall come from the presence of the Lord; and he shall send Jesus Christ, which was before preached unto you" (Acts 3:19, 20).

We must pray for this gift until we have total assurance of our right standing with God on the basis of faith in Christ's merits alone. Without doubt, the greatest prerequisite to receiving the latter rain is not perfection, as we used to believe and teach, but that we recognize our sinfulness and need for Christ's covering robe of righteousness. If we don't detect a true need for it, then we will never agonize in prayer to have it. And that means we will be unprepared to endure the time of trouble that still looms ahead.

THE TIME OF TROUBLE

The time of trouble begins as Jesus finishes His priestly duties in the courts above. "At that time shall Michael stand up, the great prince which standeth for the children of thy people: and there shall be a time of trouble, such as never was since there was a nation even to that same time: and at that time thy people shall be delivered, everyone that shall be found written in the book" (Dan. 12:1). Thankfully the passage ends with a wonderful promise that God will deliver His people when Jesus returns to earth.

Our purpose of reviewing the time of trouble is not to incite fear but rather to inspire hope and confidence that God is willing and able to take care of His own. Moreover, we want to find out the secret of the saints' victory over the forces of evil at the end of time. It will assure us of triumph during this worst moment of earth's history.

Earlier we learned that the latter rain was a knowledge that salvation comes through faith in Christ's saving merits alone. God's people sense their guilt and unworthiness, and now they trust in His forgiveness to cover their defects. They realize their Lord's merciful character and have learned to trust Him as a child does a loving father. Notice that this experience is what prepares them to face the time of trouble. "When the third angel's message closes, mercy no longer pleads for the guilty inhabitants of the earth. The people of God have accomplished their work. They have received 'the latter rain,' 'the refreshing from the presence of the Lord,' and they are prepared for the trying hour before them" (*The Great Controversy*, p. 613).

Scripture also refers to the time of trouble as "the time of Jacob's trouble" (Jer. 30:7). Ellen White gives us special insight into the experience that God's people will go through during this time by reviewing the night that Jacob wrestled with the Angel when he faced destruction from his brother Esau (please review Genesis 32:24-30). "Jacob's night of anguish, when he wrestled in prayer for deliverance from the hand of Esau . . . , represents the experience of God's people in the time of trouble" (*ibid.,* p. 616).

The Great Controversy offers us a "play-by-play" account of both Jacob's experience and that of the saints at the end of time. I will briefly highlight the parallels between the two experiences, providing the page number from *The Great Controversy.* By comparing them, we shall be better able to discover the means by which both found victory.

Jacob's Experience

Satan stirs up Esau's anger against him (p. 616).

Jacob suffers intense anxiety, fear, and self-reproach over his sinfulness (p. 616).

He discovers that his only hope is in the mercy of God and that his only defense is prayer (p. 616).

The patriarch does everything he can to make his wrongs right to avert the danger (p. 616).

Alone before God he confesses his sin and gratefully acknowledges God's mercy (pp. 616, 617).

With deep humiliation he pleads the promises of the covenant God made to him and his fathers (p. 617).

He wrestles with a spiritual force that he thinks is an enemy (p. 617).

Jacob discovers that it is actually Christ (p. 617).

He seeks from Christ reassurance of his pardon (p. 617).

Finally he clings to the Angel, pleading for the blessing of pardon (p. 617).

The Saints' Experience

Satan stirs up the wicked against them (p. 618).

Satan presents their sins before God and the angels, claiming the right to destroy them (p. 618).

The Lord permits their confidence in His forgiveness to be severely tested (pp. 618, 619).

The saints see little good in themselves as they review their life records (p. 619).

They fully realize their unworthiness (p. 619).

Satan tries to destroy their faith in Christ's forgiveness by terrifying them with the thought that the defilement of their sin is still with them (p. 619).

The saints fear they have not repented of every sin and that their faults will negate God's promise to save them (p. 619).

They fear their defects of character will bring reproach on God's name (p. 619).

The saints feel a keen sense of self-reproach (p. 619).

They afflict their souls before God, point to their past repentance, and plead the Savior's promise to forgive (p. 619).

We see here what Jacob and the saints have in common—they both recognize their sinfulness and unworthiness, but plead God's forgiveness according to the promise of His covenant. Here is their secret to victory and deliverance.

When we discuss the issue of the 144,000 and their "overcoming," we often relate it to the realm of human achievement. But like Jacob they will experience victory only through their own defeat (see Genesis 32). Thinking to preserve himself, he enlisted all the power of his humanity to fight against the Angel. It wasn't until God defeated him—until his thigh was dislocated—that he came to realize his utter helplessness. As he cast himself on God's mercy, seeking for the imputed blessings of the Angel, the Lord pronounced Jacob an overcomer and changed his name to Israel.

Likewise, our greatest need in the end-time is to be defeated by God. Most often it is our spiritual pride in what we know or what we do for God that is our greatest obstacle to "overcoming" by a complete surrender to Jesus. But one thing is certain—either we will be broken by the message of total reliance in Christ's merits, or crushed in the judgment when heaven sees our lives in contrast to those merits. Like Jacob, when someone seeks to show us how our best efforts to be a Christian fall short of God's perfect standard, we begin to fight against the idea as though it came from the enemy. It is only as the teaching that we can obtain salvation *solely through jus-*

tification in Christ's merits paralyzes our trust in our human efforts that our characters will change and be made humble and dependent. As with Jacob, we can realize the victory that God desires to give us only through the agony of our own spiritual defeat. Only as we overcome by the blood of the Lamb do we qualify to sit with Christ in His throne (see Rev. 12:11; 3:21).

I want to be quite frank. As I travel and speak throughout the world of Adventism I feel a great concern about how we relate to the time of trouble. Some treat it as no big deal, something far off, or maybe even something that will never happen. Many have an almost presumptuous attitude that declares, "I will live however I want now, and when and if that time comes, God will take care of me." It leads them to get entangled in the ways and cares of the world and robs them of the time they need to spiritually prepare for the end.

On the other extreme is the mind-set that tells itself, "I will work real hard now to get so perfect in my life and character that I will be able to endure the time when it comes." Pessimistic, they seem to spread gloom and doom with every breath they take. Because their focus is on their own perfection, it will certainly mean that they will not be prepared for the trouble once it does arrive.

My burden is that we not fall prey to either of Satan's distractions, but will get our focus where it has to be—on Jesus and His covenant of grace! We need to learn how to trust implicitly in Christ's forgiveness. It will shield us from the self-reproach that comes from feelings of unworthiness and sinfulness. Becoming intimately acquainted with Christ's forgiveness alone will give us the key to victory, both now and in the time of trouble. This experience of exercising faith is one we are not to wait until the time of trouble to obtain, but must partake of now in preparation for the time of trouble.

Notice what Ellen White says will happen to many who delay their preparation. "Those who exercise but little faith now are in the greatest danger of falling under the power of satanic delusions and the decree to compel the conscience. And even if they endure the test they will be plunged into deeper distress and anguish in the time of trouble, *because they have never made it a habit to trust in God.* The lessons of faith which they have neglected they will be forced to learn under a terrible pressure of discouragement. . . . The 'time of trouble, such as never was,' is soon to open upon us; and we shall need an experience which we do not now possess and which many are too indolent to obtain" (*ibid.,* p. 622; italics supplied).

The devil seeks to prevent us from ever having a genuine walk with God, an experience that knows firsthand about His willingness to forgive and forget. He accomplishes this through two strategies. First, he seeks to keep our minds absorbed in earthly matters so that we neglect the time needed with God to obtain the experience. I call it the Valium approach to dealing with our sense of need. We seek anything and everything we can to forget the fact that we are sinful and that we need Christ's forgiveness. But because we are incurably religious, we still make a profession of faith. Ellen White writes of such individuals that "they must have some means of quieting their consciences, and they seek that which is least spiritual and humiliating. What they desire is a method of forgetting God which shall pass as a method of remembering Him" (*ibid.,* p. 572). Wealth, position, honor, educational accomplishments, leisure and entertainment—whatever it takes to make us feel better about ourselves and stifle the need to repent, we will seek it.

But God knows what awaits us and that we are not prepared. So in mercy He seeks to unsettle our present comfort in an effort to bring us to our senses before it is too late. "We should now acquaint ourselves with God by proving His promises. Angels record every prayer that is earnest and sincere. We should rather dispense with selfish gratifications than neglect communion with God. The deepest poverty, the greatest self-denial, with His approval, is better than riches, honors, ease, and friendship without it. We must take time to pray. If we allow our minds to be absorbed by worldly interests, the Lord may give us time by removing from us our idols of gold, of houses, or our fertile lands" (*ibid.,* p. 622). Though I hate to say it, maybe this is what we Laodicean Americans needs most—an economic crash that will put it all in perspective for us. I have often thought that, though painful, it would be merciful of God to let it happen.

Second, the devil seeks to divert our trust in the forgiving merits of Christ by leading us to prepare for the time of trouble in a legalistic way. The idea is that if I can get perfect enough by the close of probation, then I won't require the forgiveness of Christ during the time of trouble. Absurd as this sounds, it has been an underlying school of thought among many conservative Adventists. It is easy to see how this approach sets us up for failure by causing us to try to avoid needing His forgiveness instead of learning to live in light of it.

Perhaps this second class will find themselves in the most distress during the time of trouble. Or perhaps they will be part of that class described in this statement: "When God's presence was finally withdrawn from the Jewish nation, priests and people knew it not. Though under the control of Satan, and swayed by the most horrible and malignant passions, they still regarded themselves as the chosen of God" (*ibid.*, p. 615). One thing is certain—at that time when they finally sense that they are not perfect but still sinful, they will either collapse under the reality of the fact or seek to deny it through their religious pretensions.

Legalists need to learn now, before probation closes, that God is not expecting absolute, perfect performance but absolute trust in the merits of Christ to save them "from the wrath to come" (1 Thess. 1:10). They must learn the divine principle stated in the book *Steps to Christ* that says the closer we come to Jesus, the more sinful we will appear in our own eyes (p. 64). This principle is not temporary, but eternal. Even during our intimate relationship with Jesus in heaven we will have a deep sense of the fact that we were not saved by any worthiness within ourselves, but by His grace. As with Jacob who wrestled with the Angel because His presence made him feel insecure, so perfectionists will surely wrestle with the Spirit of grace that comes to show them their need. They will think it an enemy and try to resist it. Viewing them as weakness, legalists have trouble facing failure and defeat.

But those growing in grace see their failures as divine opportunities to develop trust in grace (see Micah 7:7-10). It reminds us of Thomas Edison's response to the question of whether or not it was true that he had nearly 2,000 failures before he finally invented the lightbulb filament. He answered that he had experienced no failures but had nearly 2,000 successes in discovering what didn't work.

That's why the true children of God know nothing of defeat and can never be defeated. They have learned how to overcome themselves and their defects by the "blood of the Lamb" (Rev. 12:11). And as with Jacob, it will be said of them: "He had power over the angel, and prevailed" (Hosea 12:4).

Here is the key to overcoming both now and during the last days. This is real spiritual warfare—to fight our tangible imperfections with an unseen promise. It will happen no differently with us than it did with Jacob. "Satan endeavored to force upon him a sense of his guilt in order to discourage him and break his hold upon God. Jacob was driven almost to despair; but he knew that without help from heaven he must perish. He had sincerely repented of his great sin, and he appealed to the mercy of God" (*The Great Controversy*, p. 618).

May God grant to us the spiritual wisdom that will enable us to "come boldly unto the throne of grace, that we may obtain mercy, and find grace to help in time of need" (Heb. 4:16).

A SHAKING OVER CHURCH ISSUES

Chapter 9

THE EARTH WAS LIGHTENED WITH HIS GLORY

Without question the Lord has blessed the Seventh-day Adventist Church with great truth for the end-time. Its divine commission is to take this marvelous light "into all the world" (Mark 16:15) and deliver it to the doorstep of every "nation, and kindred, and tongue, and people" (Rev. 14:6). But it is going to take more than human wisdom and human effort for the church to fulfill its mission. Even today, with the great worldwide explosion of evangelism our church is experiencing, we are still falling far short in reaching the earth's masses.

The Adventist Church is increasingly acquiring the theological components and organizational structures that will enable it to set the world ablaze with the knowledge of God. Yet compared to the church in apostolic times, it lacks the needed power of the Holy Spirit. Only by means of the latter-rain Spirit will the end-time church finally fulfill its commission by lighting the earth with the glory of God (see Rev. 18:1). The final impetus will be "not by might, nor by [human] power, but by my spirit, saith the Lord of hosts" (Zech. 4:6). Without the Spirit the church is no more effective than a car without fuel.

The church is God's government on earth. As with His government in heaven, the Lord has ordained that His earthly government operate on the principle of the golden rule. It is God's purpose to forever implant this life-changing principle into the lives of individual members. As we discussed earlier, this happens as individual members have a solid experience in reflecting Christ's mercy to others. When this takes place the church will become transformed and by the power of the Holy Spirit rapidly complete its task. Notice the simple condition upon which God has promised us this divine energy: "When those who profess the name of Christ shall practice the principles of the golden rule, the same power will attend the gospel as in apostolic times" (*Thoughts From the Mount of Blessing,* p. 137).

But in a practical sense how do we live the golden rule? The apostle Paul laid out its principle to the Philippians when he told them: "Make me truly happy by agreeing wholeheartedly with each other, loving one another, and working together with one heart and purpose. Don't be selfish; don't live to make a good impression on others. Be humble, thinking of others as better than yourself. Don't think only about your own affairs, but be interested in others, too, and what they are doing" (Phil. 2:2-4, NLT). Then he proceeded to give them the example of Christ, pointing out how He didn't consider His own reputation when He came to live and die in our place. "Let this mind be in you," Paul said, "which was also in Christ Jesus" (verse 5).

Like the Philippians, we too need to get our attention off ourselves and onto the needs and interests of others. Most of us in the church today are so worried about being right that we end up unconsciously doing wrong before the Lord in the way we treat each other. The sum and substance of true religion is not always about being right in regards to what is truth, but is determined by the spirit that we have toward those who are obviously doing wrong. How would we want others to treat us were we in their shoes? According to the Lord's instruction in Matthew 7:12, whatever that answer is automatically becomes our duty to them. "In your association with others, put yourself in their place. Enter into their feelings, their difficulties, their disappointments, their joys, and their sorrows. Identify yourself with them, and then do to them as, were you to exchange with them, you would wish them to deal with you. This is the true rule of honesty. . . . It is a principle of heaven, and will be developed in all who are fitted for its holy companionship" (*Thoughts From the Mount of Blessing,* pp. 134, 135). Here is golden-rule living at its best. If we want to know what heaven is really like, we need go no further than this.

The Lord wants each of us to incorporate the principle into our own experience. He desires that we learn it so well that it actually becomes second nature to us. Therefore, He has provided real situations for us down here to provide us plenty of opportunities for practice. God brings us into constant contact with fellow humanity. But more vitally, He guides the interaction in the home and church in order for us to get more intense training. He arranges it so that we shall constantly encounter people who do not think and act the same way we do. By this means He seeks to develop a Christlike mind and attitude within us. To love the unlovely, to encourage the most hopeless, to become supportive of those whom we disagree with—this is our great challenge. To become like Jesus and have "compassion on the ignorant, and on them that are out of the way," is the experience that should be sought by all who name the name of Christ (Heb. 5:2).

BY THIS SHALL ALL MEN KNOW . . .

In the end it will be by this means that the world will know that we have been with Jesus, who so perfectly identified with us despite our unloveliness. The fact that we possess correct doctrinal truths will not impress others with the fact that we have authentic religion nearly as much as will the way in which we treat one another. It will be just as Jesus said it would: "By this shall all men know that ye are my disciples, if ye have love one to another" (John 13:35). In fact, this is the truest test of whether or not we have really been converted. "We know that we have passed from death unto life, because we love the brethren. He that loveth not his brother abideth in death" (1 John 3:14). And please, let's not be so naive as to think that John was referring here only to those who agree with us. On the contrary. The real test is to love those who get under your skin the most! But it must be done, in each one of us.

Oh, may the Spirit of the living God break our hard and unfeeling hearts of stone. Otherwise we, who think we know so much of the truth, will be the most surprised in the end to find out that we have done nothing more than deceive our own selves. "It is the greatest and most fatal deception to suppose that a man can have faith unto life eternal, without possessing Christlike love for his brethren" (*The Seventh-day Adventist Bible Commentary,* Ellen G. White Comments, vol. 5, p. 1141).

Any group of people, be it the home or the church, that practices the golden rule will enjoy a unifying experience and breathe the very oxygen of heaven. This does not necessarily mean that each member will see eye to eye on every point. But it does require that each will have been humbled under the instruction of the Holy Spirit to the point where they honestly "esteem [others] better than themselves" (Phil. 2:3). They will cease to view their own ideas, convictions, and experience, even though they have evidence that their beliefs are grounded in truth, as the criterion for everyone else. Instead, they will be most eager to point all to the life of Jesus Christ and allow them the religious liberty to develop their own personal copy of that pattern. Jesus is "the way, the truth, and the life" (John 14:6)—not us.

Many of us read something from inspired writings and become convinced it is truth that some in the church have neglected. Automatically we become zealous to bring everyone else around to accept our new conviction. Thus we create issues that Satan uses to cause divisions, pitting conservatives against liberals and liberals against conservatives. As walls of opinionated pride rise, Jesus weeps. We begin relating to each other as the enemy instead of pursuing the course our Lord did toward Judas by all the more becoming his servant. Yet we justify our attitudes and actions on the basis that we think we are right and possess the standard of truth. We usually even have inspired statements that we think justify our course of action. But the Lord speaks to us from that golden-rule city and tells us that in the end what it all finally boils down to is that "the standard of the golden rule is the true standard of Christianity; anything short of it is a deception" (*Thoughts From the Mount of Blessing,* pp. 136, 137).

In this context, the very truths that God intended to unify us, the devil now employs to divide and destroy. The cause of truth becomes a stumbling block, not only to those who reject its presentation, but as with the religious leaders of old, also to them who possess it. Many today will allow their perceptions of what they think is right to make them critical, thus blunting their affections and sympathies for those who oppose them (*ibid.,* p. 123). It is impossible for such individuals to become like Christ through golden-rule living. Jesus put it this way in speaking of our times: "And because iniquity shall abound, the love of many shall wax cold" (Matt. 24:12).

"Rebellion and apostasy are in the very air we breathe" (*The Seventh-day Adventist Bible Commentary,* Ellen G. White Comments, vol. 1, p. 1114). No matter where we go we shall feel the presence of apostasy. And it's only going to get worse. Our great challenge will be to remain within that strained marriage relationship or home or church environment in which iniquity abounds, and endure unto the end until we become like Jesus in our response to those we perceive as erring ones. When we become truly settled into the truth ourselves, we will not become so easily unnerved by what we see going on around us.

Does this mean then that we should never share our convictions of what truth is? Of course not. The development of truth has always come about by the agitation produced by its presentation. But we need to be extremely guarded in how we communicate what we believe to be right so that it doesn't come across in a haughty manner that oppresses and condemns those who might not agree with our ideas.

The courteous nature of the golden rule forbids us to engage in a campaign to tear others down so as to build ourselves up. "Insinuations, words that hurt the reputation of one who is doing the Lord's work, grieve and dishonor the Saviour. . . . Unless you cease encouraging evil speaking, unless you guard as Christians the reputation of your fellow workers, you will endanger your own soul and the souls of many others. No longer talk about the wrong that someone is doing. Never, never repeat a scandal. Go to the one assailed, and ask him in regard to the matter. God has not appointed any man to be the judge of another man's motives and work. He who feels at liberty to dissect the character of another, he who intentionally detracts from the influence of a fellow worker, is as verily breaking God's law as if he openly disregarded the Sabbath of the fourth commandment" (*Review and Herald,* May 12, 1903).

Those who come in line with the spirit of God's golden rule law will cease to oppress the consciences of others by forcing truth upon them. To do so is to develop into another beast power that resorts to measures that God Himself has pledged never to use. It was this lesson—to unlearn the use of force and develop the art of leading—that Moses took 40 years to acquire as he herded sheep. God calls people the sheep of His pasture, and sheep can only be led, not forced.

Jesus referred to this when He said: "And I, if I be lifted up from the earth, will draw all men unto me" (John 12:32). It is God's desire that we present truth, be it in the form of theological doctrine or some visible behavioral standard, in the most attractive manner possible so as to draw, by reason of their own free will, all who come in contact with it. This is how God would have us carry out the work of reformation among us. "Reformers are not destroyers. They will never seek to ruin those who do not harmonize with their plans and assimilate to them. Reformers must advance, not retreat. They must be decided, firm, resolute, unflinching; but firmness must not degenerate into a domineering spirit. God desires to have all who serve Him firm as a rock where principle is concerned, but meek and lowly of heart, as was Christ. Then, abiding in Christ, they can do the work He would do were He in their place. A rude, condemnatory spirit is not essential to heroism in the reforms for this time. All selfish methods in the service of God are an abomination in His sight" (*Testimonies for the Church,* vol. 6, p. 151).

Chapter 10

SATAN'S DISUNIFYING EFFORTS

The time has come when everything that can be shaken will be shaken. We are in the shaking time. Be assured that only those who live the prayer of Christ for unity among His disciples, working it out in practical life, will stand the test" (*Review and Herald,* June 18, 1901).

Satan fully understands that Seventh-day Adventist unity threatens his plans. Therefore, he works relentlessly to create and maintain a climate of disunity throughout church ranks. At every attempt by God to unite His people, Satan intervenes to urge upon the church his counterfeits. But in the end the church will be united upon one foundation of truth—Christ's saving righteousness. Many will rise up against it, claiming the church has gravitated toward error. It will lead them to break ranks with the church whom they view as being in apostasy. In fact, this process is already taking place.

Proverbs 11:14 declares: "Where no counsel is, the people fall: but in the multitude of counselors there is safety." Notwithstanding this ancient instruction, though, multiple groups and individuals, both on the conservative and liberal ends of the theological spectrum, have tried to promote their particular views of what truth is within Adventism. But the organized body saw no light in what they

103

felt so strongly about. Because their views do not carry the weight within the church that they feel they should, many have either left the fellowship of the church or are currently on their way out.

Ellen White wrote about such a class: "Many do not realize the sacredness of church relationship and are loath to submit to restraint and discipline. Their course of action shows that they exalt their own judgment above that of the united church, and they are not careful to guard themselves lest they encourage a spirit of opposition to its voice. Those who hold responsible positions in the church may have faults in common with other people and may err in their decisions; but notwithstanding this, the church of Christ on earth has given to them an authority that cannot be lightly esteemed. . . . Church relationship is not to be lightly canceled; yet when the path of some professed followers of Christ is crossed, or when their voice has not the controlling influence which they think it deserves, they will threaten to leave the church. True, in leaving the church they would themselves be the greatest sufferers; for in withdrawing beyond the pale of its influence, they subject themselves to the full temptations of the world" (*Testimonies for the Church,* vol. 4, pp. 17, 18).

Such attitudes are nothing new. Before any of us were ever born, Ellen White wrote to a man who had involved himself in extreme teachings that the church would not endorse. "You will take passages in the Testimonies that speak of the close of probation, of the shaking among God's people, and you will talk of a coming out from this people of a purer, holier people that will arise. Now all this pleases the enemy. We should not needlessly take a course that will make differences or create dissension. We should not give the impression that if our particular ideas are not followed, it is because the ministers are lacking in comprehension and in faith, and are walking in darkness" (*Notebook Leaflets From the Elmshaven Library,* vol. 1, p. 110).

Even today, though, people still from time to time blindly ignore her counsel. As a result, they often end up denouncing the Adventist Church as Babylon. Others may not go to that extreme, but if their course involves taking tithe money that otherwise would have gone into the church treasury, they participate in similar results (see *Testimonies to Ministers and Gospel Workers,* p. 53). Though they may continue to view themselves as faithful Seventh-day Adventists, in essence they have set up in a separate organization that tends to work against the church. The result is always disunity, never unity.

Actually, zealous individuals can undermine church unity, though they may not openly denounce it or steal from its treasuries. Anything, whether by individuals or organized ministries, that weakens the faith of the people in the organized church, thereby setting themselves up as "centers of influence" to which people must come in order to understand divine mysteries, is following the same path that Lucifer walked in the heavenly courts. They are like Absalom who "stole the hearts of . . . Israel" (2 Sam. 15:6).

Most often it involves differences of theology that people have with the mainstream denomination. They publicly promote their views through their sermons, videos, and self-created newsletters. Though they sincerely assume that they are doing a great work for God, denominational history reveals that they are in reality blinded by the archdeceiver and end up working against God's will. The ditches along the Advent highway are strewn with such wandering individuals.

But how can we avoid the same thing happening to us? Are there any guidelines that the Lord has given to prevent us from getting caught up in such false movements? The key is to trust that God is at the helm and is leading in the organized Seventh-day Adventist Church. Notice that it's through the organized church that God advances truth, not through people and ministries who work independently of the organization. "No such thing is countenanced as one man's starting out upon his own individual responsibility and advocating what views he chooses, irrespective of the judgment of the church. God has bestowed the highest power under heaven upon His church. It is the voice of God in His united people in church capacity which is to be respected" (*Testimonies for the Church,* vol. 1, pp. 450, 451).

This suspicious lack of trust among our members in what the corporate body teaches forcibly impressed itself upon my mind recently. One evening I visited a church elder and his wife. The husband, in his search for truth, had read a number of publications distributed by various independent groups. During our discussion he quizzed me how I felt about what different independent ministers taught. Being very open with him, I soon found that I had some major disagreements with nearly every theory he presented. After a while his exasperated wife asked me, "Well, Keavin, is there anybody you do theologically agree with?" (I guess to her I was starting to look pretty haughty and like a know-it-all myself!) All I could respond with was "Sure there is. I agree with the views that have been adopted and taught by the church."

HUMBLE OPINIONS

Many of our people are inclined to believe that God is going to work through some offshoot group instead of the organization that He has so carefully raised up. They do so because these groups plant seeds of distrust toward the church and its leaders in the minds of those who listen to them. Then they build themselves up by contrasting their views with what they have convinced others to be denominational error.

This sowing of distrust toward God's established church government echoes the doubt the serpent raised in Eve's mind. Sadly, it is how such factions gain their followers. Because the groups have to resort to attacking the church in order to advance their own cause, isn't it evidence in itself that they really don't have truth? The bottom line of the whole matter is that "it is the want of deference for the opinions of the church that causes so much trouble among brethren" (*ibid., vol. 5, p. 107*). The key word here is deference. Noah Webster stated: "We often decline acting in opposition to those for whose wisdom we have a great deference" (*Webster's Dictionary* [1828]).

I am not suggesting that we should allow others in the church to be our minds. No! We are all to be like the Bereans who studied to know for themselves what was truth. It is the first and highest responsibility of every church member to investigate the gospel issues and make their own determination what the truth is. All I'm trying to bring out is two points.

First, as we approach the study of truth we must remember that "God has made His church a channel of light, and through it He communicates His purposes and His will. He does not give one an experience independent of the church. He does not give one man a knowledge of His will for the entire church, while the church, Christ's body, is left in darkness" (*Testimonies for the Church,* vol. 3, p. 414). Instead of drawing premature conclusions as to why they are wrong, we need to give corporate views a fair, respectful hearing and then go from there.

Oftentimes the first introduction to our minds of a hot button theological question comes from a well-prepared presentation from a disaffected mind. If we accept that initial viewpoint we become biased against any other view and are more likely to entrench ourselves into that one way of looking at things. Such minds become dwarfed and incapable of growth. But "those who sincerely desire truth will not be reluctant to lay open their positions for investigation and criticism, and will not be annoyed if their opinions and ideas are crossed" (*Counsels to Writers and Editors,* p. 37). "No true doctrine will lose anything by close investigation" (*ibid.,* p. 35).

Second, if after we have objectively studied out the issues we still conclude that the church is wrong, we must not feel at liberty to make our differences prominent if it will endanger the unity for which God is laboring in the church. By this I'm not saying it's wrong to make public our views. The problem arises when we become so adamant that we become unwilling to honestly consider anyone else's. Furthermore, we denounce anything that opposes what we believe and by our headstrong course we feel justified in creating disunity among God's people.

Notice how Ellen White taught this concept: "The Reformation was greatly retarded by making prominent differences on some points of faith and each party holding tenaciously to those things where they differed. We shall see eye to eye erelong, but to become firm and consider it your duty to present your views in decided opposition to the faith or truth as it has been taught by us as a people, is a mistake, and will result in harm, and only harm, as in the days of Martin Luther. Begin to draw apart and feel at liberty to express your ideas without reference to the views of your brethren [the body of believers], and a state of things will be introduced that you do not dream of. My husband had some ideas on some points differing from the views taken by his brethren. I was shown that however true his views were, God did not call for him to put them in front before his brethren and create differences of ideas. . . . When these contentions come in before the people, they will think one has the argument, and then that another directly opposed has the argument. The poor people become confused" (*The Ellen G. White 1888 Materials,* pp. 23-25).

Does this not accurately describe the state of confusion brought about in our church today by the unwise actions of some among us? Undoubtedly many will read this divinely inspired counsel, and yet because they believe so strongly that God has raised them up to set the church aright, they will disregard it and continue to cause confusion and disunity. "Oh, how Satan would rejoice if he could succeed in his efforts to get in among this people and disorganize the work at a time when thorough organization is essential and will be the greatest power to keep out spurious uprisings and to refute claims not endorsed by the Word of God" (*Testimonies for the Church,* vol. 9, pp. 257, 258).

If we take seriously Christ's prayer for unity among His disciples, we will reveal that same spirit through our actions and our attitudes. "We are coming to a time when more than ever before, we shall need to press together, to labor unitedly. In union there is strength. In discord and disunion there is only weakness. God never designed that one man, or four, or twenty, should take an important work into their own hands, and carry it forward independently of other workers in the cause. God wants His people to counsel together, to be a united church, in Christ a perfect whole. . . . No one company is to form a confederacy, and say, 'We are going to take this work and carry it on in our own way; and if it does not go as we want it to, we will not give our influence to have it go at all.' This is Satan's voice, not God's. Do not obey such suggestions" (*Selected Messages,* book 1, p. 374).

A LIGHT IN A DARK PLACE

Regarding the theological positions of the church, we will each have to draw our own conclusions. For nearly 18 years I have studied our church's theological tenets. I have also given fair considera-tion to differing views from both conservative and liberal voices within Adventism. My conclusion is that the basic doctrinal theol-ogy of the mainstream denomination is more solid than even our pi-oneers realized. The foundations of our faith, contrary to the belief of some among us, are sovereignly intact and are but waiting to be more clearly defined. They are now in the final stages of preparation for us to deliver to the world in a loud cry.

Jesus' vigilance hasn't failed. The essential elements of gospel truth are in the church. But there are some colorful nuances and ar-rangements of these gospel gems that He will, as He attempted to do in 1888 through the united body of the church, cause to make an impact that they have not heretofore produced. Also, certain gems of truth will one day take on still greater luster and promi-nence. We haven't appreciated them as God knows they need to be in order to move our souls into that deep, settled love for Him. Such love will characterize the experience of those who are finally filled with latter-rain power.

The only thing now lacking is a church composed of gracious members, who being moved by gospel reality, have consequently put away all selfish agendas of wanting to be the prominent voice in the church. We've yet to humbly submit to the beneficent authority of heaven that God gave, and still maintains in, this organized people.

The entire universe is eagerly waiting for us to lay aside our po-litical differences and other side issues that only cause divisions among us, and instead focus on doing what God has raised us up to do—that is, to present Christ and His law to the world in the con-text of the three angels' messages. "Of all professing Christians, Seventh-day Adventists should be foremost in uplifting Christ before the world. The proclamation of the third angel's message calls for the presentation of the Sabbath truth. This truth, with others included in the message, is to be proclaimed; but the great center of attrac-tion, Christ Jesus, must not be left out" (*Gospel Workers,* p. 156).

This will take place as we come to understand more about the unique role Jesus plays in the plan of salvation. As with the church at Pentecost, the humbling effects of the Holy Spirit as He presents to our minds the merits of Christ will regenerate every one of us who crowds into the upper room. We will be eternally enamored with the person of Jesus Christ and His merits to justify us. "The end is near! We have not a moment to lose! Light is to shine forth from God's people in clear, distinct rays, bringing Jesus before the churches and before the world. . . . One interest will prevail, one subject will swallow up every other—Christ our righteousness" (*Review and Herald,* Dec. 23, 1890). Only then can the bride unite with the Spirit in giving the world an invitation to "come" and "take the water of life [Christ] freely" (Rev. 22:17).

When we understand the full significance of Christ's role ourselves, its contagious influence will be felt not only by the inhabitants of our world, but by the universe as well. The earthly church is the arena that God has chosen for the principles of His heavenly government to be played out in and demonstrated before the entire universe. "The church is God's appointed agency for the salvation of men. It was organized for service, and its mission is to carry the gospel to the world. From the beginning it has been God's plan that through His church shall be reflected to the world His fullness and His sufficiency. The members of the church, those whom He has called out of darkness into His marvelous light, are to show forth His glory. The church is the repository of the riches of the grace of Christ; and through the church will eventually be made manifest, even to 'the principalities and powers in heavenly places,' the final and full display of the love of God" (*The Acts of the Apostles,* p. 9; see also Eph. 3:9, 10).

Yet today many look with discouragement upon the condition of our own church and wonder how God is ever going to pull off within it the greatest demonstration of His kingdom that will ever be made to the universe. They regard it as full of theological perversions, lowered standards, and the justification of open sin. Eager to see righteousness done in the land, such individuals are sometimes zealous in their efforts to make it happen.

But we must understand God's deeper purpose for allowing sin and apostasy to exist within our ranks. It's the identical principle by which He has been operating ever since the controversy between good and evil first started. He permits apostasy to develop to maturity as a means of purifying the church, just as He did with the heavenly church. As wrong becomes popular in the church the hearts of many are revealed in that they gravitate toward it. And we may confidently expect to witness in the future, as we have in the past, that all movements within the church based on erroneous assumptions will eventually separate from it. All this will mature and culminate in the Sunday-law crisis. Ellen White tells us that at that time "the church may appear as about to fall, but it does not fall. It remains, while the sinners in Zion will be sifted out" (*Selected Messages,* book 2, p. 380).

God has stated again and again that He is going to purify His remnant church and through it make His eternal purposes known not only to our world, but to the entire universe. And we may be sure that "God's purposes know no haste and no delay" (*The Desire of Ages,* p. 32). We will find ourselves tested as we by faith believe that God's purposes in dealing with His church are right on time. It will be one of our greatest challenges to synchronize our hopes to His timing. But one thing is certain—soon the sad, final shaking will have done its work and a people will develop through whom the cause of Christ will triumph through His unified church.

Chapter 11

A WHOLE LOT
OF SHAKING GOING ON

The history of our world repeatedly reveals that differences in opinion between religious denominations can cause major dissension and even bloodshed. Perhaps at no other time was this more evident than during the Protestant Reformation. It was an age when ideological preaching caused multitudes to leave the medieval religion of Rome, ushering in one of the most marked shaking periods in human history.

The greatest leader of that Reformation was Martin Luther. Though most of his views were theological in nature, one of the more controversial positions he advocated was against the church's unscriptural demand for a celibate lifestyle for priests and nuns. In a small pamphlet that soon began to circulate within Europe's monasteries and convents he exposed the practice as an unbiblical tradition. Then in 1523 nine nuns read the pamphlet and became convicted that they had been misled in taking their vows. Wanting out of their religious order, they requested Luther's help in escaping from the convent. Luther responded by hiring two men to smuggle the women to freedom. Then he had the nuns dropped off, one by one, at designated Protestant households throughout Germany. The last one, Katherina von Bora, lodged with members of Luther's congregation in Wittenburg.

As time passed Luther and Katherina married. News of the event drew heavy criticism from Luther's enemies. " 'It is incest,' exclaimed Henry VIII. 'A monk has married a vestal,' said some. 'Antichrist will be the offspring of such a union,' said others; 'for a prophecy announces that he will be born of a monk and a nun.' To this Erasmus [a defendant of Luther's] replied with a sarcastic smile: 'If the prophecy is true, what thousands of antichrists already exist in the world!' " (J. M. Merle D'Aubigne, *History of the Reformation,* p. 388).

MODERN-DAY REFORMATION?

Historically, Seventh-day Adventists have had their disagreements with the Roman Church and its defenders. Part of this stems from our understanding of the role it has played in Bible prophecy. But at the same time an unhealthy, almost unchristian, attitude has developed among some associated with the Adventist Church. They go out of their way to attack the Catholic Church publicly. In the past decade we have witnessed such misguided labors as billboards and advertisements in national papers denouncing the pope and his church.

Those who take this aggressive course often view themselves as modern-day reformers. But should we seek to imitate the aggressiveness of earlier reformers as we address our theological and prophetic differences with those churches outside Adventism? "Men who are harsh and censorious often excuse or try to justify their lack of Christian politeness because some of the Reformers worked with such a spirit, and they claim that the work for this time requires the same spirit; but this is not so. . . . While ministers of Christ must denounce sin and ungodliness, impurity and falsehood, while they are sometimes called to rebuke iniquity among the high as well as the low, showing them that the indignation of God will fall upon the transgressors of His law, yet they should not be overbearing or tyrannical; they should manifest kindness and love, a spirit to save rather than to destroy" (*Testimonies for the Church, vol. 4,* p. 486). One thing is certain—never should we discuss papal power and organization until we have first led our audience to a clear understanding of its role as revealed in the prophecies of Daniel and Revelation. Such a course will only cause us to appear as intolerant, arbitrary bigots.

The counsel Ellen White gave concerning how Adventists should deal with the sensitive issue of racial prejudice in the American South during the latter part of the nineteenth century might be appropriate for how we should publicly address the errors of other religious powers. "As time advances, and opposition strengthens, circumstances warn us that discretion is the better part of valor" (*Testimonies for the Church,* vol. 9, p. 205). Heroism in our day will not display itself by lashing others with our pens or tongues. On the contrary, it will involve getting truth across to people with the least amount of public offense.

It is vital that we realize the depth of Paul's teaching to the Ephesians that "our fight is not against human foes, but against cosmic powers, against the authorities and potentates of this dark world, against the superhuman forces of evil in the heavens" (Eph. 6:12, NEB). I have been amazed to learn that some Adventists maintain that God could not possibly save any pope. Such individuals condemn the office of the pope for its claim to act for God on earth and then turn right around and usurp the prerogatives of God themselves by taking on the job of judgment. Can popes be saved? Absolutely! If they honestly live up to all the light they have, then they are as justified as Adventists who live up to all the light they have.

However, this does not change the fact that a cosmic war plays itself out through human religious systems. It is also a fact that an individual may be fully committed to God and still be ignorantly used to fulfill the devil's purposes. This is true of any of us, be we Adventists, Catholics, Baptists, or whatever. Peter illustrated this fact when he unadvisedly spoke for Satan while sincerely seeking to follow Jesus (Matt. 16:22, 23).

We Adventists should be extra cautious as we proceed with our divinely commissioned work. God has entrusted us with truths essential for this time. Our success depends as much on *how* we share as it does *what* we share. The human mind is easily prejudiced. That's why Jesus said to be wise as serpents and harmless as doves. People must be convinced that we are friends who have their best interest in mind rather than enemies who have come to attack what they believe.

I'm not talking here about denying truth but how we should go about discreetly presenting it. A climate has developed today in American society that seems to be highly sensitive when it comes to questioning another's religious beliefs. For instance, while it was "in vogue" to publicly attack Catholicism in Ellen White's day, this no longer holds true. George W. Bush found that out during his quest for the presidency when he went to Bob Jones University (a school noted for its public denunciation of Roman Catholicism) for a simple campaign speech in 2000. Just by going there and failing to address the issue of the school's anti-Catholicism, it placed an automatic stigma upon him in the minds of many Americans. He received so much bad press that he later made a public apology for the whole episode.

Perhaps it was because Ellen White foresaw this mind-set developing that she penned a hundred years ago these counsels to our writers and editors:

• "Let not those who write for our papers make unkind thrusts and allusions that will certainly do harm, and that will hedge up the way and hinder us from doing the work that we should do in order to reach all classes, the Catholics included" (*Counsels to Writers and Editors,* p. 60).

• "This message [Isaiah 58:1] must be given, but while it must be given, we should be careful not to thrust and crowd and condemn those who have not had the light that we have. We should not go out of our way to make hard thrusts at the Catholics. Among the Catholics there are many who are most conscientious Christians, and who walk in all the light that shines upon them, and God will work in their behalf" (*ibid.,* p. 63).

• "Let all be guarded in their words, lest they place those not of our faith in deadly opposition against us, and give Satan an opportunity to use the unadvised words to hedge up our way. . . . Our work is to study to weed out of all our discourses everything that savors of retaliation and defiance and making a drive against churches and individuals, because this is not Christ's way and method" (*ibid.,* p. 64).

• "I feel hurt when I see that so many decided thrusts are made against the Catholics. Preach the truth, but restrain the words which show a harsh spirit; for such words cannot help or enlighten any-one" *(ibid.)*.

- "We may have less to say in some lines, in regard to the Roman power and the papacy, but we should call attention to what the prophets and apostles have written under the inspiration of the Spirit of God" *(ibid.,* p. 65).

We should be especially careful when it comes to stating things that are likely to end up in the press. I thought George Reid, director of the Biblical Research Institute at the General Conference of Seventh-day Adventists, did an excellent job when in 1996 the public spotlight hit him. An Associated Press story appeared in newspapers all over the country. My local paper's headline read: "Adventist Book Calls Pope the Devil's Ally."

It was all a reaction to a portion of the book *Bible Readings,* which outlines our understanding of the Papacy's prophetic role. Student literature evangelists had distributed the book across America that summer. Catholic and Protestant leaders alike condemned Adventists for applying the prophecies of the antichrist to the papal organization. In particular, one scholar of a Protestant denomination went on the offensive. He refuted the view set forth in our publication and contacted the General Conference for an official statement. Denominational leadership assigned Reid to answer the question. When asked if Adventists indeed believe the papal office is the antichrist, Reid responded: "That's what every major leader of the Protestant Reformation believed and taught." Here is an excellent example of how we can avoid undue prejudice and still share what we believe the Bible teaches.

I myself have had intense struggles as to how to walk this fine line. The statement "We may have less to say in some lines, in regard to the Roman power and the papacy" has caused me much bewilderment. Why would Ellen White say this? It seems logical to me that the closer the Papacy comes to fulfilling its prophesied agenda, the more we would point out that fact. In an attempt to clarify what she meant, I began to ask how other Adventist writers and evangelists understood it. One well-known writer said he thought we would have less to say about the Papacy because we would have more to say about the Protestants. This may be true to some degree, but it still didn't satisfy me.

The best answer I received was from someone who told me, "I think in the future we will have less to say about the Papacy because we will have more to say about Jesus!" I believe the individual has hit the nail on the head. As I have thought about it, I am convinced that something has gone wrong with our evangelistic philosophy when we are more eager to make known what the pope is doing than what Jesus is doing. Both may have to be talked about, but the point is which one has center stage in our presentations.

Make no mistake about it—what we have believed and taught concerning religious movements in the last days will—and already is—taking place. In the years since the Second Vatican Council the Protestant churches have been making a steady retreat back to the medieval church, just as Ellen White said they would (see *The Great Controversy,* pp. 566, 588). It is amazing what they have been willing to concede.

In 1998 some Lutheran leaders signed a document modifying the position their founder Martin Luther took with the papal church over the core issue of the Reformation—justification by faith. *Time* magazine reported the landmark decision this way: "A Half-Millennium Rift: Lutherans and Catholics reach agreement on the issue that once split Western Christianity in two" (*Time,* July 6, 1998, p. 80).

Once again I am now convinced that the issue of justification by faith—that is to say, how a person is saved—will be the major issue when the final shaking really gets going. If I'm understanding the prophecies correctly, as the Protestant churches come more and more in line with the medieval view of justification by faith and works, Adventists, who have traditionally been more works-oriented, will take their stand clearly on the fact that we are justified by faith in Christ's merits alone. And many people who are in what we Adventists refer to as Babylon (those churches who hold erroneous biblical doctrines) will respond to our emphasis on the righteousness of Christ as the only hope of ever being made right with God. They will, in due time, leave Babylon to take their stand with those who

117

promote the law and the gospel in a balanced way.

My wife and I saw an example of this recently when we met a retired Lutheran seminary teacher and his wife in a buffet line. My wife asked them how they felt about the Lutheran Church's decision to seek common ground on justification. The professor's wife immediately replied, "I think it's the most wonderful thing that has ever happened in our church." Her husband said nothing.

As the couple made their way from the line to their seats, the professor left his wife's side and swung by our table. He leaned over and said to my wife, "I think there are a lot of questions that have yet to be answered!"

Inspiration tells us that when the crisis hits, multitudes in Babylon will shake off the shackles of personal relationships and affiliations within their families and churches and take their stand with the truth.

THE PURPOSE OF THE CHURCH

During my secular years I listened to a song named "Dust in the Wind." Its message was that our life and everything we do on earth is only temporary. The lyrics declared that nothing can last forever except the earth and sky.

As a Christian I would modify part of the message it portrays. First, the only thing that lasts forever is Jesus, His eternal kingdom, and those humans who choose to be a part of that kingdom. Even our present earth and sky, the only things the song said would endure forever, will also someday pass away.

So why do I bring the song up? Because it emphasizes a point that we Adventists need to acknowledge—that everything on our present world is temporary, including our church as we now know it. I say this to put things in perspective. When we get involved in building up the organizational structure of God's church on earth, we run the risk of thinking that it is going to somehow last forever. But the structure of the Adventist Church and its related institutions (schools, churches, publishing houses, hospitals, missions, administrative boards, etc.) is also temporary. Like Solomon's great kingdom, it too will eventually vanish.

History teaches us that when we get to the place where we trust too much in earthly organizations, God intervenes to show us just how impermanent such things are. That's what the fires in Battle Creek that destroyed the publishing house and sanitarium were all about. Adventists had become too dependent on what they had built in that little Michigan city. They focused their resources more on maintaining their monolithic institutions than in advancing the work of Christ on new horizons. Adventists felt secure in Battle Creek. Like Nebuchadnezzar, many felt, "Is this not great Battle Creek which we have built [with the Lord's help, of course]?" So the Lord removed it from them, forcing them to scatter into other parts of the world. As a result, God's work expanded.

It's vitally important that we understand the nature of the world-wide denomination we are constructing today. The purpose of its organizational structure is not to prove how important or successful Seventh-day Adventists can become, or how we compare to other churches, but to facilitate the spreading of the gospel message of Jesus Christ.

The church is like scaffolding used to place a brick facing on a several-story building. The scaffolding is an aid in getting the job done, not its central object. When the last brick is laid and we want to show the finished work at the grand opening, the scaffolding comes down. It has served its humble purpose and is no longer needed.

Likewise, the scaffolds of our denominational organization exist only to facilitate the completion of the gospel commission on earth. Is the present church organization important? Of course it is! How else are you going to lay brick on a seven-story building? In our metaphor each brick represents a person brought to Christ. Remember, this is the only thing that will last forever—the eternal relationship between Jesus and those saved.

After we have succeeded in bringing Christ to the attention of every person living on earth and everyone has made their eternal decision, the church scaffolding will have served its purpose and can come down. Persecution will set in, and the world will outlaw God's people. We will enter into the time of trouble. No organization will then be needed, because God has completed His work on earth. The seed will have been sown and brought to fruition. The only thing left will be for Jesus to come with His sickle and garner the harvest.

With this broader picture of the church's purpose in mind we can better detect the error of many who advocate dismounting the church now. Because they focus on the imperfections of the church, they come to believe God cannot use it. But they fail to see the perfect work the church is accomplishing—the channel that Christ works through to save human beings. Others become so fixated on the organized church that they relate to it as though it can save them in and of itself. (Isn't that one of the points we disagree with Catholicism over?) Both camps have focused on the scaffolding and not on the real work (of Christ) it is accomplishing.

Once again, the church only brings to people the message of salvation through Christ. It saves no one by itself. Neither does the church have to be perfect to accomplish its work. I've seen some pretty shaky scaffolding that still got the job done. Those who become impatient, demanding a perfect church, will be disappointed and eventually become so disoriented that they will be shaken out and leave the organized church. Because they wanted a perfect church, a perfect spouse, perfect children, they sought to seize control in obtaining such things through human force. They played God in the lives of others and in the end messed up God's intent through their impatience. Oh, how we need to learn to wait for that perfect environment. But only when Jesus comes will we have it!

Sure, when real trouble comes, when governments outlaw our religion, the face of our organized church will no doubt change. But until then we will have to work with a faulty, imperfect church, because that is all God has given us.

COME OUT OF HER, MY PEOPLE

Some Adventists have developed a superstitious fear toward spiritual Babylon. We face a real danger of becoming so sheltered within the borders of our own denomination that we lose our ability to relate to those who attend other churches. Such paranoia will prevent us from mingling with and witnessing to people who are searching for truth we possess.

I was reminded of this fact several years ago while working as the director for a small evangelistic training school. We had just completed renovations on a classroom building, and I began searching for an older-looking pulpit to match the decor. I found one in a storage room of a local Adventist church and then approached the church board and offered to buy the pulpit. During the board's discussion I learned that the church had purchased the pulpit years earlier from a Presbyterian church in town. As this fact surfaced the head elder turned to me and said, "You don't want that pulpit then."

"Why not?" I asked.

"Because it came from Babylon."

Just then one of the board members declared, "Larry, we all came from Babylon! Let the man have the pulpit!"

It's important for us Adventists to remember that as human beings we are no better, no holier, no more gifted, than people in other churches. But because of what we know, we do run the risk of viewing ourselves as an elite group and people in the other churches as inferior. The result will be the same as those Jews who developed a superiority complex toward the Gentiles. Our capacity to reach people for Jesus will thereby diminish. In the end we will be humiliated to discover what Israel also did in their relationship to the Gentile world: "God is no respecter of persons" (Acts 10:34).

The shaking will be a time of intense interaction between churches and denominations. It will be imperative that during this time we keep our focus on our mission. When the shaking really gets going we will be tempted to attack other churches. But that is not our commission. Our job is to uplift Jesus as Lord and Savior. We can then leave the results with God. As we present Jesus as the truth, the way, and the life, the sins and errors of Babylon will become evident to all willing to see them. As a result, we will witness a powerful and marked exodus from churches that have incorporated teachings that lead away from a total dependency on Christ.

Also we must be prepared for the ramifications of exalting Christ to His rightful place. It will stir up the ravening wolf nature of Satan and all who have chosen to follow him. Persecution such as we cannot now imagine will converge upon our church. It is then that God will separate the wheat from the chaff in the church. Any among us who have not clearly understood the prominent role that Jesus plays in the plan of salvation, and made this truth central in our Christian experience, will be shaken out of the ranks of God's people.

Jesus told a parable to this effect in John 10. He portrayed Himself as the shepherd who gave His life for the sheep and stated that it was only through Him that anyone could enter the door of eternal life. Christ said that if anyone tried to get there by any other way than through Him, "the same is a thief and a robber" (John 10:1). Then He talked about a time when the wolf would attempt to destroy the flock. "I am the good shepherd: the good shepherd giveth his life for the sheep. But he that is an hireling, and not the shepherd, whose own the sheep are not, seeth the wolf coming, and leaveth the sheep, and fleeth: and the wolf catcheth them, and scattereth the sheep. The hireling fleeth, because he is a hireling, and careth not for the sheep" (verses 11-13).

Right now the Adventist Church is having unprecedented success. But as happened in Jesus' earthly ministry, it will suddenly give way to unprecedented persecution. We too shall meet our crucifixion, and our church may appear as about to fall, even though it won't (*Selected Messages,* book 2, p. 380). The experience will test our individual commitment to Christ to the uttermost. If we are going to stand at that time, "we must be divested of our self-righteousness and arrayed in the righteousness of Christ" *(ibid.).*

Those who have been in ministry for pay, power, or self-glory will at that time leave. They are mere hirelings. When hard times come to a farm and there is no money, hirelings go elsewhere to find work. But the son of the owner stays because he has invested his whole life in that farm. The more difficult the circumstances, the harder he works. It will be the same for those who have expended their all in helping the church fulfill its commission to make Christ known to all the world. Though confronted with unimaginable challenges, they will refuse to yield their faith.

Ellen White wrote: "The time is not far distant when the test will come to every soul. The mark of the beast [the wolf] will be urged upon us. Those who have step by step yielded to worldly demands and conformed to worldly customs will not find it a hard matter to yield to the powers that be, rather than subject themselves to derision, insult, threatened imprisonment, and death. The contest is between the commandments of God and the commandments of men. In this time the gold will be separated from the dross in the church. True godliness will be clearly distinguished from the appearance and tinsel of it. Many a star that we have admired for its brilliancy will then go out in darkness. Chaff like a cloud will be borne away on the wind, even from places where we see only floors of rich wheat [in other words, those whom we saw as true Christians will then prove false—and notice why!]. All who assume the ornaments of the sanctuary, *but are not clothed with Christ's righteousness,* will appear in the shame of their own nakedness" (*Testimonies for the Church,* vol. 5, p. 81; italics supplied).

Again, it all comes back around to Jesus Christ and His righteousness. This is the vital message we have to give to those in Babylon. Though Ellen White declared that the Seventh-day Adventist Church was not a part of Babylon, the truth is that our church has Babylonians in it, because they are trusting in the merits of their own self-righteousness rather than in Christ's righteousness. On the other hand, churches that we define as Babylon have countless people who trust in Jesus with all their hearts. They are humble children of the King and in due time will respond to the call of Christ to "come out of her, my people" (Rev. 18:4).

It is a truth that we must settle into not only intellectually, but spiritually as well (see *The Seventh-day Adventist Bible Commentary,* Ellen G. White Comments, vol. 4, p. 1161). As we discussed in an earlier chapter, this message of Christ's saving merits is the sealing message. It is the thing we will need most when a whole lot of shaking starts going on.

Chapter 12

THE UNSEEN TOILER

n an earlier chapter we considered the time God will bathe the entire earth with His glory (see Rev. 18:1). We might naturally jump to the conclusion that it means that He will make a big show so as to catch everyone's attention. But can we be sure that it is going to happen that way? At the Savior's first advent the Bible tells us that angels proclaimed to the earth God's glory, yet only a few shepherds were in tune with their song. Most of the earth's inhabitants remained unaware that God's glory had arrived. Could it be that it will happen in a similar way at the end of time?

Most of us know about Ellen White's prophecy that when the latter-rain power of the Holy Spirit arrives, it will fall all around without some people discerning it (*Testimonies to Ministers and Gospel Workers*, p. 507). Elsewhere she predicts that at the time when the Father audibly tells His children of the day and hour of Jesus' coming, the wicked will not understand His words (*Early Writings*, pp. 285, 286). The Bible declares: "Now we have received, not the spirit of the world, but the spirit which is of God. . . . But the natural man receiveth not the things of the Spirit of God: for they are foolishness unto him: neither can he know them, because they are spiritually discerned" (1 Cor. 2:12-14). So we realize that only those in tune with His Spirit will know what He is doing in the last days.

I once heard a well-known preacher state that the Second Coming would be God's opportunity to show off. Please, let us get this straight: God is no show-off. In fact, He dwells and operates so much behind the scenes that unless we are spiritually awake, we will not discern Him. God has warned us not to make graven images, because His image is invisible (Col. 1:15). That's what He wants us to "see" about Him and His kingdom. Yet we can discern it only as we are born from above.

Phillips Brooks sought to make this point in his hymn "O Little Town of Bethlehem" when he wrote:

"How silently, how silently the wondrous gift is given!
So God imparts to human hearts the blessings of His heaven.
No ear may hear His coming; but in this world of sin,
Where meek souls will receive Him still, the dear Christ
    enters in."

God does things not to be seen but to bless. His glory reveals itself through His obscurity, His invisible and imperceptible working. While we may see the more obvious evidences of His working, the vast majority of God's endeavors go unnoticed and unappreciated, such as the food that grows to bountifully bless our tables.

We should never conclude that just because we may not observe the Lord at work He is not doing anything. Nor is God trying to play hide-and-seek with us. It's just that He operates on a drastically different wavelength than ours. Still He recognizes that some, such as Thomas, need their faith revived by clear evidences of His presence, and our golden-rule God will always meet their needs.

RIGHTEOUSNESS IN OBSCURITY

When He did have to make Himself visible He came arrayed not in the pomp and splendor of Solomon, but rather as a meek and lowly Galilean. Or when John the Baptist announced to those who had gathered at the river, "Behold, the Lamb of God," none discerned whom he spoke of, even though Jesus was right in their midst. "Jesus did not respond to the Baptist's announcement of Him, but mingled with the disciples of John, giving no outward evidence of His special work, and taking no measures to bring Himself to notice" (*The Desire of Ages,* p. 137).

It was the same way in which God has presented Himself to the prophets through the ages. "The works of Christ not only declared Him to be the Messiah, but showed in what manner His kingdom was to be established. To John was opened the same truth that had come to Elijah in the desert, when 'a great and strong wind rent the mountains, and brake in pieces the rocks before the Lord; but the Lord was not in the wind: and after the wind an earthquake; but the Lord was not in the earthquake: and after the earthquake a fire; but the Lord was not in the fire:' and after the fire, God spoke to the prophet by a still, small voice. 1 Kings 19:11, 12. So Jesus was to do His work, not by the overturning of thrones and kingdoms, not with pomp and outward display, but through speaking to the hearts of men by a life of mercy and self-sacrifice. *The kingdom of God comes not with outward show.* It comes through the gentleness of the inspiration of His Word, through the inward working of His Spirit, the fellowship of the soul with Him who is its life" (*The Ministry of Healing,* p. 36; italics supplied).

This is the revelation of God's glory that we need so desperately to see, for by beholding it we shall become changed into that same image. Our human nature makes us want to exalt ourselves. But we need to be preparing for that time when "every valley shall be exalted, and every mountain and hill shall be made low" (Isa. 40:4). Then "whosoever shall exalt himself shall be abased; and he that shall humble himself shall be exalted" (Matt. 23:12).

Here Scripture presents two groups and the effect the shaking will have upon them. The message of salvation through Christ's merits alone, apart from any accomplishment they can perform in the Lord's behalf, will lead the one group to humble themselves in His sight (see James 4:10). The gospel causes them to realize they have no advantage over anyone else, that God does not play any favorites. They consider all their righteous deeds, performed by the power of the Lord's Spirit, as mere "filthy rags" (Isa. 64:6; *Selected Messages,* book 1, p. 344). God's people won't take the attitude that whatever they are doing for the Lord is greater than what others can accomplish, because a revelation of the work Jesus did has left them humbled. Each one understands what Jesus meant when He said: "When you obey me you should say, 'We are not worthy of praise. We are servants who have simply done our duty'" (Luke 17:10, NLT).

The other class is exactly the opposite, though it is not evident to themselves in their self-blinded state. Though they profess Christ, they are really absorbed with themselves. The same spirit of vanity that often plagues the world's celebrities also infects these who try to establish their self-worth through their success in working for God. Because they are engaged in the important mission of advancing God's kingdom, they have unconsciously developed a sense of self-importance. To put it bluntly, they are self-exalted through their own estimates of self-righteousness. Self-righteousness is the result of the sinner not having a clear view of his or her own condition, as contrasted to who and what Jesus is.

Speaking of this class, the prophet Isaiah wrote: "The lofty looks of man shall be humbled, and the haughtiness of men shall be bowed down, and the Lord alone shall be exalted in that day. For the day of the Lord of hosts shall be upon every one that is proud and lofty, and upon every one that is lifted up; and he shall be brought low" (Isa. 2:11, 12). Then he adds: "Cease ye from man, whose breath is in his nostrils: for wherein is he to be accounted of?" (verse 22).

Ellen White delivered a similar message of the results of self-righteousness in the time of the shaking. "Our faith cannot be vested in any man. We need Christ's righteousness. We need Jesus ever by our side. He is our rock. It is by His might [merits] that we conquer, and by His righteousness that we are saved. When I see men exalted and praised, extolled as almost infallible, I know that there must come a terrible shaking" (*Manuscript Releases,* vol. 11, p. 91). "It is now too late in the day for men to please and glorify themselves. Ministers of God, it is too late to be contending for the supremacy. . . . It is a day when instead of lifting up their souls in self-sufficiency, ministers and people should be confessing their sins before God and one another" (*Review and Herald,* Dec. 24, 1889).

"We have no great men among us, and none need try to make

themselves what they are not, remarkable men. It is not wisdom for a single individual to strike out as though he had some great talent, as though he were a Moody or a Sankey" (*Evangelism,* p. 134).

Though it is obvious that God wants us to have humble opinions of ourselves and our work, we have still found a way to let our pride flourish. Adventism has developed its own jet set of celebrities whose word some people hang onto as though it were straight from God. I'm not intimating that these people are bad—just simply trying to point out a danger that lurks close by. Those who see themselves as superior to others will not survive the last shaking of our church. At that time an army of "unknowns" will surface to fight faithfully and humbly the Lord's cause. "In the last solemn work few great men will be engaged. They are self-sufficient, independent of God, and He cannot use them. The Lord has faithful servants, who in the shaking, testing time will be disclosed to view" (*Testimonies for the Church,* pp. 80, 81). Those individuals and ministries who somehow have come to believe that God has especially raised them up, and that the finishing of His work on earth depends upon them, will definitely someday take a fall.

As we near the end Satan will increasingly tempt us to exalt ourselves. We may know a lot in the area of theology; we may be a highly successful evangelist; we may be the president of a conference or the head elder of a large church; but whoever or whatever we are, if we think more of ourselves than we ought, we will certainly fail when God's final shaking spreads throughout the ranks of Adventism. An old saying still proves true in our modern times: "When little men cast long shadows, it is a sure sign their sun is about to set."

"There will be an army of steadfast believers who will stand firm as a rock through the last test. But where in that army are those who have been standard-bearers? Where are those whose voices have sounded in proclaiming the truth to the sinning? Some of them are not there. We look for them; but in the time of the shaking they have been unable to stand, and have passed over to the enemy's ranks. Christ says to him who feels his weakness, 'Let him take hold of my strength [that is, His saving merits], that he may make peace with me, and he shall make peace with me'" (*Sermons and Talks,* vol. 1, pp. 88, 89).

Things are really no different now than they were when Jesus came to reveal His Father's glory. "The Pharisees sought distinction by their scrupulous ceremonialism, and the ostentation of their worship and charities. They proved their zeal for religion by making it the theme of discussion. Disputes between opposing sects were loud and long, and it was not unusual to hear on the streets [or in the Sabbath schools] the voice of angry controversy from learned doctors of the law. In marked contrast to all this was the life of Jesus. In that life no noisy disputation, no ostentatious worship, no act to gain applause, was ever witnessed. Christ was hid in God, and God was revealed in the character of His Son. To this revelation Jesus desired the minds of the people to be directed, and their homage to be given. The Sun of Righteousness did not burst upon the world in splendor, to dazzle the senses with His glory. It is written of Christ, 'His going forth is prepared as the morning.' Hosea 6:3. Quietly and gently the daylight breaks upon the earth, dispelling the shadow of darkness, and waking the world to life. So did the Sun of Righteousness arise, 'with healing in his wings.' Mal. 4:2" (*The Desire of Ages,* p. 261). The fact that Jesus didn't reveal His glory in the way the people of that day expected was one of the major reasons they would not accept Him as the Messiah (see *The Sanctified Life,* p. 14).

We are safe only as we have a right view of God's character. Here in the end there are "gods many and lords many" just as inspiration told it would be (*Testimonies for the Church,* vol. 5, p. 80). Everywhere we turn, opinions of what people think God is flash from pulpits, books, and the air waves. Only those who discover His true image and conform to it by constantly beholding it in the midst of apostasy will be a part of the church privileged to reveal that same unassuming, glorious character to the world. He still bids us today: "Learn of me; for I am meek and lowly in heart: and ye shall find rest unto your souls" (Matt. 11:29). It's the identical lesson that Christ was endeavoring to teach Nicodemus when He compared God to the wind. He said that "the wind bloweth where it listeth, and thou hearest the sound thereof, but canst not tell whence it cometh, and whither it goeth: so is every one that is born of the Spirit" (John 3:8). Yes, we too are to be born again into an invisible, godly influence in this world.

Each time we lose sight of Him and His humility we put ourselves in grave danger. "In our separation from God, in our pride and darkness, we are constantly seeking to elevate ourselves, and we forget that lowliness of mind is power" (*Testimonies for the Church,* vol. 3, p. 477). The deciding factor for each one of us in the great struggle between God and Satan will be whether or not we have found Christ and learned of Him. "All self-exaltation and self-admiration are the result of ignorance of God and of Jesus Christ, whom He has sent. How quickly will self-esteem die, and pride be humbled in the dust, when we view the matchless charms of the character of Christ! The holiness of His character is reflected by all who serve Him in spirit and in truth" (*The Seventh-day Adventist Bible Commentary,* Ellen G. White Comments, vol. 4, p. 1178). "The whole gospel is comprised in learning of Christ, His meekness and lowliness" (*Testimonies to Ministers and Gospel Workers,* p. 456).

THE UNKNOWN TOILERS

The key here is not just in knowing what to expect to see in God, but also what He looks for in us. Satan tells many that the greater and more noticeable their work for God is, the more representative they will be of Him. May we never forget that God is not swayed by the things that awe humanity. The man who gave a large offering didn't impress Him nearly as much as did the little widow who sought to give her pittance secretly (Mark 12:41-44). As God's people, we need to learn and never forget this truth about Him. "We need a calm waiting upon God. The need of this is imperious. It is not the noise and bustle we make in the world which proves our usefulness. See how silently God works! We do not hear the noise of His steps, and yet He is walking about us, laboring for our good. Jesus did not seek for notoriety; His life-giving virtue was going out to the needy and the afflicted through silent actions, whose influence extended far into all countries and was felt and expressed in the life of millions of human beings. Those who desire to labor with God have need of His

Spirit every day; they need to walk and labor in meekness and humility of spirit, without seeking to accomplish extraordinary things, satisfied to do the work before them and doing it faithfully. Men may not see or appreciate their efforts, but the names of these faithful children of God are written in heaven among the noblest workers, as scattering His seed in view of a glorious harvest. 'Ye shall know them by their fruits'" (*The Seventh-day Adventist Bible Commentary,* Ellen G. White Comments, vol. 4, p. 1144).

We don't see things the way God does. In God's estimation the person who washes and prepares the Communion cups is doing as important a work as does our denomination's most successful and well-known evangelist. "Not the amount of labor performed or its visible results but the spirit in which the work is done makes it of value with God" (*Christ's Object Lessons,* p. 397). Yes, my brothers and sisters, Jesus still identifies Himself "with the world's unknown toilers" (*Education,* p. 77).

Let us forever fix it humbly but firmly in our minds that God's last demonstration of truth will be one of the most awesome manifestations of divine glory that the universe will have ever witnessed. Yet it will go by unnoticed by a large portion of earth's inhabitants, some of whom have spent their entire lives within the borders of the Adventist Church. It will be accomplished through a group of silent, gentle servants, "hidden ones" who are now in obscurity within the remnant church as well as His faithful ones who now reside in the obscurity of Babylon. Through them God will exhibit the final, humble display of Himself to the world (*Testimonies for the Church,* vol. 5, pp. 80-82).

Those two groups are now being imperceptibly formed within the church. Today it is just as it was long ago when the church congregated down at the Jordan to hear John. "Eyes that had never been turned in faith to Him that is invisible beheld not the revelation of the glory of God; ears that had never listened to His voice heard not the words of witness. So it is now. Often the presence of Christ and the ministering angels is manifest in the assemblies of the people, and yet there are many who know it not. They discern nothing unusual. But to some the Saviour's presence is revealed. Peace and joy animate their hearts. They are comforted, encouraged, and blessed" (*The Desire of Ages,* p. 136). No doubt some of them will be among that meek and lowly group that heaven employs to light the world with the glory of God's kingdom.

THE HUMBLE CHURCH

God's ultimate purpose and calling of His church is to reflect His humble principles to a world given over to self-glorification. For this reason He has promised to be with it and protect it until the very end of time. Though we may often see things happening within the church that shake our confidence that God is leading it, we should always remember that God has already taken that all into consideration, and the fact it is happening is only because God sees it as best to allow it. Remember, Elijah in his high-profile role failed to see 7,000 devout worshipers of the invisible God.

Though He may be the unseen toiler, His toiling is unceasing for His people. "Through centuries of persecution, conflict, and darkness, God has sustained His church. Not one cloud has fallen upon it that He has not prepared for; not one opposing force has risen to counterwork His work that He has not foreseen. All has taken place as He predicted. He has not left His church forsaken, but has traced in prophetic declarations what would occur, and that which His Spirit inspired the prophets to foretell has been brought about. All His purposes will be fulfilled" (*The Acts of the Apostles,* pp. 11, 12).

May we all come to rest in the fact that God's divine purposes for His church are right on time and will one day ultimately be fulfilled. To it God will fulfill the promise that "the Gentiles shall come to thy light [our presentation of Jesus Christ], and kings to the brightness of thy rising" (Isa. 60:3).

CONCLUSION

The purpose of *Surviving the Shaking* has been to prepare its readers for the end-time. I have sought to do this by showing how God has placed the prophetic gift in the church so as to equip His people with a right experience through right theology.

It is vital that we understand the relationship between the prophetic gift, the church, and the message. The purpose of the church is to herald the message of Christ's righteousness—as it relates to the immutability of God's law—to the world. The prophetic gift guides and aids the church in its mission. In conclusion, I would like to focus on the end result of God's communication (through the prophets) of His message (of mercy and justice) with His people (the church).

In my first endeavor to explore the subject of the shaking, I compared the two cleansings by Jesus of the Temple in Jerusalem to two cleansings that take place in the Adventist Church (see *The Shaking Among God's People* [Hagerstown, Md.: Review and Herald Pub. Assn., 1994], p. 45). I based that analogy on a statement I had found in *Testimonies for the Church,* volume 9, page 228: "God's love for His church is infinite. His care over His heritage is unceasing. He suffers no affliction to come upon the church but such as is essential for her purification, her present and eternal good. He will purify His church, even as He purified the temple at the beginning and close of His ministry on earth."

Just as Christ cleansed His Temple's courts at the beginning of His earthly ministry, He later cleansed the Adventist movement through the disappointment of 1844. Now, just as He cleansed His Temple on earth a second time near the close of His ministry, He will again purge the ranks of Adventism, as well as the Christian church at large (which God cleansed in its infancy at Calvary). But I want us to take a closer look at the nature of that cleansing. By doing so, we shall see what it is that the Lord so earnestly wants to do to prepare us for when the time comes for "the removing of those things that are shaken . . . that those things which cannot be shaken may remain" (Heb. 12:27).

The biblical history of God's dealings with His people reveals that everyone who claims the name of Christ will face an ultimate test of their profession. It will separate the tares from the wheat. By God's grace we have received probationary time to prepare for it. During this period we must learn of God's character and by His Spirit reflect it in our own experience. If we don't, we will fail when our testing time comes.

The events surrounding Calvary were the test for Christ's followers in their day. There we saw the love of John, the vacillation of Peter, the doubt of Thomas, and the failure of Judas. But they were only a few of the people who had their faith tested there. A whole nation came face to face with God at Golgotha. We don't know them all by name, but some passed the test; others failed.

However, I want to examine one group in particular. They were those who did not flee when Jesus had earlier cleansed the Temple. Well aware of their needs that day, they did not leave when Jesus chastised the money changers and Temple officials. When those whose proud and arrogant presence had defiled it hastily fled the Temple, these people became the recipients of Jesus' tender compassion and healing sympathy. That day He made an unfading impression on their minds about God's character. As a result, they allowed the Holy Spirit to reproduce in them that same spirit of compassion and sympathy for the needs of others. The seeds sown by the Savior that day in the lives of those who were dying for want of sympathy bore fruit within some of those same people when Jesus went to Calvary. *The Desire of Ages* speaks of some of those whom Christ had healed in the Temple: "At the crucifixion of Christ, those who had thus been healed did not join with the rabble throng in crying, 'Crucify Him, crucify Him.' Their sympathies were with Jesus; for they had felt His great sympathy and wonderful power. They knew Him to be their Saviour; for He had given them health of body and soul. They listened to the preaching of the apostles, and the entrance of God's Word into their hearts gave them understanding. *They became agents of God's mercy, and instruments of His salvation*" (p. 163; italics supplied).

I suggest that the only way we are going to be able to face the trials and tests before us, in a practical sense, is likewise to develop a sympathetic character toward those with whom we come into contact. Unless we become Christlike in character, how are we ever going to represent Him to the world? The only way we can dispense mercy is first to receive it. That's what it means to have an experience in the gospel, to receive the forgiveness of God to the point at which it makes you ready and willing to forgive. Jesus seemed to make this a mandate for salvation when He said: "For if ye forgive men their trespasses, your heavenly Father will also forgive you: but if ye forgive not men their trespasses, neither will your Father forgive your trespasses" (Matt. 6:14, 15). If we fail to grant others the mercy that we ourselves have received, we become like the Dead Sea, where water flows in but nothing flows out.

I must confess that as I review my life I find where I have failed miserably at this. I realize that I must ask God's forgiveness for my unforgiveness toward others. Both in my home and in my church I have failed in giving an example of God's forgiving and merciful character. I have been too quick to judge, and too slow to forget the wrongs of others. I have hurt others at the very time when I could have healed them. I long for the day when God's Spirit shall change this spirit both in me and in my church.

It's not really all that hard—in theory, that is. Rather, it's the transformation of an intellectual knowledge to life experience that's the real challenge. And it's a process that takes a lifetime to complete. But it's God's will to do this for us, as He stated in His promise: "A new heart also will I give you, and a new spirit will I put within you: and I will take away the stony heart out of your flesh, and I will give you an heart of flesh" (Eze. 36:26). This process of replacing our hard hearts toward others with feelings of mercy and compassion is the real essence of what it means to have the image of God restored in us.

Without a doubt this will be our greatest test—to love the unlovable for Christ's sake. Ellen White put it plainly: "When the religion of Christ is most held in contempt, when His law is most despised, then should our zeal be the warmest and our courage and firmness the most unflinching. To stand in defense of truth and righteousness when the majority forsake us, to fight the battles of the Lord when champions are few—this will be our test. At this time we must gather warmth from the coldness of others, courage from their cowardice, and loyalty from their treason" (*Testimonies for the Church,* vol. 5, p. 136).

The only way we can ever arrive at such a high calling is to saturate ourselves in the mercy and forgiveness God has shown toward us to the point at which it transforms our attitude toward others. We may not possess a degree in theology or hold a prominent position in the church, but if this gospel change occurs in our heart, we qualify for the promise of Christ: "Blessed are the merciful: for they shall obtain mercy" (Matt. 5:7). If we obtain such an experience, then God knows that nothing can shake us.